DECORATING
with PAINT

ABOVE Many shades of stippled red glaze, plus tinted
varnish, create a gorgeous depth of lacquered colour which
is particularly glamorous lit up at night.

PREVIOUS PAGE Artist John Fisher paints cut-out portraits in
the style of the old 'silent companions' sometimes seen
standing in a corner, or in front of the fireplace, in paintings
of rooms from Jacobean times onwards. By using
photographs, he was able to portray a vivid likeness of me.

DECORATING
with PAINT

How to Create Decorative Surfaces with Trompe l'Oeil, Stencil,
Spatter, Marble, Lacquer, Stipple and Sponge Techniques

JOCASTA INNES

Harmony Books
New York

CONTENTS

C O N T E N T S

INTRODUCTION

When I first began writing about decorative paint finishes five years ago, the subject was one of limited interest. Apart from exclusive decorating firms, which incorporated a discreet use of decorative techniques like dragging and marbling into their house style, and a few little-known centres for instruction in 'fantasy' finishes along the lines of the Isabel O'Neil studio in New York, hardly anyone seemed to have heard of those outlandish phrases I used to drop experimentally, such as 'scumble' or 'rag-rolling'. I had been on the trail of tinted glazes or 'transparent paint', especially in its DIY application, for several years – in fact, ever since the day I found a couple of painters racing up and down ladders, putting lilac glaze over dove-grey, in a house that I was visiting. I felt this was a discovery that ought to interest everyone who had become bored with flat emulsion and gloss white, and I was sure that if they could be shown how distinguished and attractive distressed or broken colour could look, and how subtly it could be used to remedy the sort of problems most DIY decorators face, there could hardly fail to be some response. Despite my faith in the subject, I was as astonished as anyone else when my first book, *Paint Magic*, found itself in the best-seller list.

Decorative painting was already sophisticated in ancient Egypt, as shown in this tomb painting of hunting fowl in the marshes at Thebes.
Tapestries have always been luxuries, but cheaper alternatives have existed – painted canvas hangings or 'water works', like this ravishing seventeenth-century example from a Gloucestershire manor house.

The ideas in my book were not new – nearly all discoveries in interior design are re-discoveries – and all I had done was to research the decorative techniques I found most appealing and describe how to apply them. The real innovation was in telling an old story to a new audience – the sophisticated end of the DIY market. The fact that stylized marbling and graining are found on Mycenaean pottery of 2200 BC shows just how old the story is. In ancient Egypt, where timber was scarce, realistic fake graining, complete with knots and characteristic figuring, was being produced by the Third and Fourth Dynasties. Egyptian furniture was painted, gilded and stencilled. Fresco decoration, where a range of lime-resistant colours were applied to wet lime plaster, was highly developed by Roman times, as the murals at Pompeii show.

Specialized paint effects went in and out of fashion through history in response to the predominant mood in interior decoration, which, in its turn, was affected by broader cultural trends and the economic climate. By the time I came to write about them, decorative finishes had been generally out of favour for almost a century, though a robust vernacular tradition of graining and marbling persisted in pub décor. My own explanation for the success of the decorative paint revival is that it has coincided with a growing appetite for colour and pattern in reaction to the bland neutrality of 'Scandowegian' (shorthand for Scandinavian-influenced design) and the ascetic sparseness of the Modern Movement, which between them inhibited delight in colour and texture in favour of 'form'.

The idea adopted most enthusiastically of all has undoubtedly been the tinted glaze. Manipulated while still wet, glazes can be used to create a dizzy array of textured effects from pintucks to crushed velvet, while achieving a soft, 'see-through' quality far removed from the thick, brash, opaque colour of modern miracle paints.

ABOVE *Painted 'architecture' was already a recognised decorative device for framing murals by 79 AD, when the Hall of Mysteries was painted in Pompeii.*

LEFT *The Entrance Hall at Saltram, grand and formal, illustrates how closely the eighteenth-century neo-classicists followed the classical system of sub-dividing wall spaces to create a 'framework'.*

For centuries, the use of glazes has been standard academic practice among painters for building up flesh tints, deepening shadows and generally adding depth or luminosity to paint colours. It was John Fowler, the most inventive British decorator of this century, who pioneered the decorative uses of 'transparent paint', as he called it. Combining the delicate film of colour in a tinted glaze with the grainer's traditional techniques for imitating wood, such as stippling, combing and mottling, he opened up a wealth of fascinating possibilities. Subtle rather than showy, this transparent overpainting lent a delicate ambiguity of tone which softened and enlivened all colours, even notoriously risky interior colours, like red. Layering different transparent colours over each other gives an almost infinite range of possible effects, and a richness of nuance matched only by the exquisite fabrics of that master colourist, Fortuny, coloured with layer upon layer of transparent dye. As Gerard Manley Hopkins wrote gratefully: 'Glory be to God for dappled things.'

Not all the comments on the rash of speckled, sponged, ragged, dragged and marbled surfaces which appeared some five years ago were favourable. Rumbles of discontent emanated from the élite of professional specialist painters, who felt that all this amateur activity, with half-trained art students and eager beginners muscling in, was lowering standards and giving special finishes a bad name. Nevertheless, despite criticism and the suspicion that this new enthusiasm for special finishes might be short-lived, the notion of using paint decoratively is not only still with us, but livelier and more inventive than at any time since the mid-nineteenth century.

This book aims to show how paint finishes have developed. The state of the art has gone from strength to strength: the discreetly distressed finishes in fruit-sorbet colours that once seemed so novel are now the norm, while today the more adventurous are creating effects of much greater intensity, with richer colours and bolder patterns. However, as soon as you introduce strong colour and pattern in one area of a room, for example richly textured and coloured walls, the other room elements – ceiling, floor, woodwork, doors – cry out for similar treatment. White ceilings, white woodwork and close carpeting in plain colours, standard ingredients of interiors a decade ago, provide such a negative surround to rich wall schemes that the whole room becomes unbalanced.

It should come as no surprise, then, that leading decorative painters today receive as many commissions for special floors, ceilings and woodwork schemes as they do for walls. The late Geoffrey Bennison was a recognized master of this kind of polychromatic approach, piling on effects with a simultaneous grasp of both the detail and the broad sweep. Jean and Mark Hornak, two of the most imaginative decorative painters, developed some of their most exciting ideas under Geoffrey's guidance; marbled woodwork containing the sudden visual surprise of boldly striped 'agate', a painted ceiling showering flowers as vividly precise as those in a Dutch still life, subtly wood-grained doors and shutters which stencil artist Mary MacCarthy then elaborates with marquetry designs inspired by seventeenth-century Dutch furniture. These effects, splendid taken singly, are quite breathtaking when matched with equal bravura in wall finishes, curtains, furnishings, floors and lighting.

Another decorative trend which is emerging strongly, and which gives today's rooms a more energetic, virile look, is the use of boldly patterned graining on doors and woodwork. In keeping with the current vogue for Biedermeier furniture, decorator Victoria Waymouth has designed a room with immaculate blond sycamore graining on all the woodwork, dramatized by a sleek black fillet which echoes the customary Biedermeier inlay of ebony or ebonized fruit wood. The same house runs a gamut of spectacular grained finishes, each chosen to complement a particular room – pale ivory 'camembert box', streaked with silvery grain marks, is used for one room, mahogany for double doors with gilt mouldings, burr maple for an amazing casket-like bathroom. The magic of such expert finishes is that they give a convincing and luxurious look to the most unprepossessing, if practical, materials like fibreboard, chipboard and ply.

Another effect which is becoming popular imitates the time-weathered patina of painted walls seen in Italy, where earthy ochres and siennas blend into each other to create a warm overall glow. This is a look that can be achieved by various different means and methods. I have seen a whole range of techniques used – colour rubbed in finely like rouge, thick colour sanded off to leave a freckle embedded in the surface, pink plaster with artificial cracks crayonned in and then varnished with orange shellac to give a burnished sheen, or watercolours worked on in layers. Another way to give walls patina is with traditional materials, now unexpectedly fashionable again. The extraordinary 'antiqued' finish invented by Jim Smart, doyen of the trade, uses dry colour over gesso and French chalk. Distemper – another revival – combines whiting and glue size for a powdery texture which is fragile compared with modern vinyl emulsions, but gives wonderful chalky colours. Designer and antique dealer, Leonard Lassalle, finds distemper an ideal wall finish in the old beamed houses in his part of Kent. He uses odd muted lilacs, greygreens and ochre-yellows, and sometimes paints a wall black as a background to a dramatic painted wall design in egg tempera, based on early crewel-work (see pp. 96–7, 112–3).

For a real showstopper, however, murals and trompe l'œil (painted decoration so realistic as briefly to deceive the eye) are hard to beat. Not since the Renaissance have so many clients commissioned so many ambitious wall decorations, and a showpiece painted by one of the famous 'muralisers', such as Lincoln Taber, Ian Cairnie or Richard Shirley Smith, is an international status symbol. Clients may choose a mural of a romantic Italian garden or an exotic jungle scene to surround an indoor swimming pool, a stylized oriental landscape for a stairway, or the ruins of Petra for a bathroom. But painted illusion need not be so elaborate. One of the simpler notions, a 'sky' ceiling, painted blue with drifting white clouds, is so much in demand that a decorative painter could easily make his living on skies alone, were it not for the back troubles which follow too much ceiling work. Painted 'stone-work', or rustication, is a favourite finish for entrance halls, lobbies and stairwells, as it gives an air of architectural consequence to uninteresting or awkward spaces. The grandest solution of all for walls that are in the wrong place is to dissolve them visually with a huge mural suggesting a classical panorama or a wooded landscape.

It is not mandatory to be a millionaire, with teams of specialist painters at your command, to enjoy such painted spectaculars; gifted amateurs can achieve great effects with time and patience. However, labour-intensive schemes such as that designed by Carlo Briganti for the room of a Parisian client are probably best avoided. He devised an intricate collage of tiny brown and tawny painted paper strips, inspired by pretty nineteenth-century straw-work called Tunbridge Ware, and it took four workers five months to paste down each strip of paper individually over the four walls.

If you cannot own a glorious old tapestry, the eighties solution is cheap and cheerful – paint one. Or, if that seems too onerous, steal a motif or two from it and stencil them onto your walls.

Stewart Walton (whose artwork illustrates this book) created a rich overall wall pattern for his own house, based on motifs from an oriental rug (see p. 108). Painted in soft colours, which vary in intensity just like an irregularly faded rug, the pattern keeps growing as time permits. Similarly, the wall design in my own kitchen grew in fits and starts, and almost everyone who came to the house helped by adding a panel or two. The bold curvaceous pattern is based on a Jacobean wall design I saw in an Essex pub, and each panel has been painted freehand, resulting in a pleasing, and human, irregularity (see p. 20).

Art critic Roger Fry, founder of the Omega group, wrote an article in 1917 called 'The Artist as Decorator' in which he imagines the artist turned house-painter. 'Now our artist may be able, merely out of the contrast of two or three pure colours applied in simple rectangular shapes, to transform a room completely, giving it a new feeling of space and dignity or richness. In fact he can underline as it were the actual proportional beauty of the architecture or counteract its architectural defectiveness.' I like to imagine the reverse of that situation, where the house-painter dares to turn decorative artist, but Fry's observations on the potency of colour and its ability to transform still stand.

As Jim Smart is fond of saying: 'A room that has been properly painted needs no furniture.' This is not to say that marbled dados, sky ceilings and ragged walls would compensate for living in empty rooms, but it serves to dramatize the importance of colour and texture as the sovereign remedies for the imperfect rooms in which most of us live.

ABOVE *Flamboyant gilded and painted chairs designed by William Burges show how a Victorian genius re-interpreted traditional decoration.*

RIGHT *William Burges was one of the few great English architects to use colour uninhibitedly, and this room designed around his furniture shows nineteenth-century polychrome decoration at its most dazzling.*

1

EXPERIMENTING WITH PAINT

PAINTABILITY AT HOME

IN MY OWN LONDON HOUSE

You might reasonably suppose that the most excitingly decorated homes would be those belonging to decorative painters themselves. People who do not earn their living by the brush assume that an expert marbler, like one of the Hornaks, must live surrounded by panels of golden sienna or white Sicilian marble, and that someone with as many skills as Susan Williams, who used to run the Colefax Studio, would have covered every inch of furniture with some lavish fantasy finish. With a few notable exceptions, the last place most painters feel inspired to work on is their own home. What strikes the amateur as challenging and fun is more often a busman's holiday for professionals who cannot help automatically costing out their brushwork, and often feel disorientated when left to their own devices, without a decorator or client imposing restrictions.

For my sitting room I devised my own rubbed-in effect,
aimed at giving a fresco texture. The blue 'framing'
sharpens up an amorphous space and ties in with a
stencilled frieze, giving the room a sort of logic. In my
bathroom I used greyed pastel colours with a honeysuckle
stencil, to which greater definition is given by
painted bands.

RIGHT *Based on a Williamsburg colour, the warm blue in my study was 'dirtied' with both burnt and raw umber. The blinds were hand-painted to pick up the carpet design.*

ABOVE *A detail of the frieze, cribbed from an Indian textile design, enlarged and re-coloured. The fat rope stencil was added later.*

Ian Cairnie, one of the more imaginative trompe l'œil artists, admits that he goes to pieces if he is not given a stylistic framework. He can paint a brilliant pastiche of a Claude Lorraine landscape or a Dutch flower painting in a few days. But, in his words, 'if you asked me to paint something in my own style I'd still be there weeks later, not knowing where to begin. I need to be given a style in which to paint.'

Many decorative painters admit to fantasies about how they would like their own homes to look, but this transformation rarely takes place. Lack of time is one excuse. Then there is the curse of sheer perfectionism, which comes of producing work to the highest standards in luxurious and beautiful surroundings. 'I'm such a perfectionist', says stenciller Mary MacCarthy, the owner of a small, pretty cottage in Norfolk, 'that everything has to be exactly right or I can't live with it. So I look at blank walls and tell myself how wonderful it will be when I finally get round to it.'

Like Mary MacCarthy, I find it hard not to give a guilty start and become apologetic when I am asked if my house is covered from top to toe 'with all those wonderful painted finishes you write about'. Seeing, analysing, and writing about so much excellent decorative work makes it easy to become over-critical, and too mindful of all the shortcomings (unfinished areas, ideas that need further development) to take in the overall effect of your own home. But when I suddenly see my place with new eyes, after a few days away somewhere, I realize all over again that it has a special atmosphere, a look of its own, and that this is due more than anything else to colour and pattern achieved with paint.

One lesson I learned in turning the dilapidated ruin I stumbled upon six years ago into the tolerably complete state it has now reached, is that an adventurous deployment of painted effects and finishes is the cheapest, most effective solution to decorating problems given that the ideal solution is usually too expensive to carry out. For instance, all the original wide, elegant cornices characteristic of Regency interiors had disappeared, except for a battered stretch left in the front hall. It would have been better practice architecturally to restore them because the proportions of period rooms depend on such details, but the cost was prohibitive so I was obliged to try and achieve a similar visual balancing act by other means. Painted or stencilled friezes, painted lines and stencilled borders in contrasting colours help to restore the balance as well as making a decorative point in their own right. I am just beginning to realize, however, after seeing some of the latest developments in painted and decorated ceilings, that for this ruse to work fully, the painted treatment needs to be extended over the ceiling as well.

The house was a near derelict shell when I bought it; ghetto-like poverty overtook Spitalfields when the silk-weaving industry collapsed in the early nineteenth century. My reason for buying it was the most persuasive one possible. I was homeless, had next to no money, and it was available, central and cheap. Even so, by the time it had been re-roofed, the windows re-made, ground floors replaced, and the back extension completely rebuilt, there was a large hole in my bank account. On the advice of friends with experience of rehabilitating 'squats', my young daughters and I began by colonizing the top floor. The moment any cash came my way, I put it towards reclaiming the cold, empty, desolate rooms below, employing tradesmen to do the skilled work, like plastering, while I, and such skilled and unskilled helpers as I could recruit, worked at those time-consuming jobs that are feasible for amateurs: burning-off thick crusts of old paint on the woodwork, pulling out nails, patching holes, sanding, filling, scraping, priming and painting.

John Fowler always recommended, and I endorse this, that you should never do anything to a new place till you have lived in it for six months. In that way you discover things not immediately apparent, but important for intelligent re-decorating: how the light falls, which rooms are sunlit and at what times, how the layout of the building works or fails to work, and what arrangements of furniture are possible. Yet anyone who has lived on a building site knows how passionately one craves an oasis of order, colours instead of endless plaster dust, textures and the illusion, at least, of a proper room. The moment the plaster had dried (and sometimes before, which has led to an unpremeditated 'old palazzo' look on the walls downstairs), I rushed in with my paints and my ideas about colour. Should anyone wonder how far I follow my own precepts, let me say that there is not a square foot of the building, except perhaps for a ceiling or two, that has not had its paint-work teased about in some way or other.

It is not that I cannot let well alone, but that I keep trying to make 'well' better. I belong to the 'organic' school of decorators, who insist that rooms and colour schemes should be allowed to grow. I find blueprint rooms, where everything has been planned on the drawing-board, unsympathetic, and as uncomfortable and constricting as clothes that are too tight. I find certain colours strongly suggest themselves for particular rooms after a while, but the great usefulness of paint techniques like glazes and washes is that they allow you to have second and third thoughts even after the colour is on the walls, if the result is not what you want – unlike wallpaper. The thundery blue which covers everything in my study except the ceiling, was a proprietary paint in a grey-blue shade which I tinted down with ultramarine stainer. On the walls, however, as often happens, the colour which looked so pretty over a small area misbehaved and looked oppressively dark, its matt surface sucking in

every ray of light. Sponging over a paler version of the original colour, lightened with white, was helpful, as was shining-up blue painted woodwork with varnish, but the saving grace of the room proved to be the wide frieze (a pattern copied from the border of an Indian cotton bedcover) painted round the room just beneath the ceiling in warm peachy colours. Blue curtains overloaded the colour yet again, so I stepped up the stencil with a second band of colours, a fat red and yellow rope, underlining the first.

I try to use paint, whether in a plain colour or as a pattern, architecturally, to help define space and correct imbalance. The blue lines that divide the walls of my sitting room, which has cloudy pinkish walls (strong red glaze rubbed to the merest veil of colour over a smooth silk vinyl), are perhaps the most successful example. The room began rosy, which was pleasant enough but rather nondescript. A stencilled frieze round the top of the walls unbalanced the room completely, emphasizing its odd shape and leaving great yawning spaces below. The idea of running coloured bands round to give the walls more definition was inspired by photographs of an apartment in New York. It took two days to complete, from measuring out to the final painting of a second layer of khaki glaze over the first blue glaze which had a softening, ageing effect – at first it looked too much like gift wrapping. The room still needs what I call 'thickening up', but the lines have helped to anchor it visually.

The most fashionable finish in my house, the low key rustication of the front hall and staircase, is the only one original to the house. I uncovered the design, printed in sepia and off-white on thick parchment-textured paper, as I scraped off the usual palimpsest of later papers, varnishes and other rubbish deposited over a century and a half. The paper was beyond rescue, so I simply copied it in paint, liking it for its demure neo-classicism and curious to see how well the original de-

ABOVE *The hand-painted block motif in my kitchen is based on one I found in an old pub. I think of it as a painted version of a 'friendship' quilt because friends add bits now and then.*

RIGHT *The very restrained painted 'stonework' in my hall reproduces the original Regency wallpaper design. The mural uses a Greek vase motif found on a matchbox cover while on holiday in Rhodes.*

corators had understood their building. Most people take to it at once, but what makes it work for me is the flash of colour beyond in a mural of running figures, which is an enlarged version of the picture on a tiny matchbox picked up on holiday in Rhodes. It was not the only Regency paint finish that I uncovered. Two more, which I decided not to reproduce, also turned up: the sitting room was stencilled with brown anthemion borders on blue paint, and one of the upstairs bedrooms was sponged in a wild medley of red and green over creamy-white, making huge wavy stripes of colour that I found decidedly unsettling.

Nearly all my furniture is junk, and much of it is painted, either to disguise its lowly origins, or change its character to suit a room, or sometimes just to try out an idea. Professional decorative painters dislike painting furniture as a rule because they cannot make a profit out of work that takes days to achieve the superlative finish needed if painted pieces are to sell. For the DIY painter with a decorative urge, on the other hand, painting furniture is a picnic, a small-scale operation that you can take up and leave off as you please and that gives just enough scope for trying out new ideas. I have experimented with nearly every style of furniture painting, from Adam's neo-classicism (to be avoided unless you are prepared to make a meticulous job of it – bodged Adam is bad news) to ethnic or folksy. My most successful pieces, I think, are those to which I gave a 'printed' look with a tiny overall stencil, or in one case (a good idea by the way) a lino-cut copy of a sixteenth-century fabric printing block.

My bedroom is the one room in the house that owes nothing to paint. The walls are stapled over with striped cotton shirting, discovered in a great bolt in the basement of a wholesale fabric shop in London's Brick Lane. I bought 50 metres at 50p a metre, which gave me more than enough to 'wall' the room completely, stapling the cotton

over thin wadding straight onto the plaster, make quilted curtains to match, and still have enough left over to run-up sheets and a duvet cover one day. But it would not be my room if signs of my ruling obsession had not begun to creep in. First, I painted the four-poster bed, made out of deal by an American friend, furniture designer and craftsman Jim Howett. Painted and varnished many times for an old japanned look, it will acquire gilded decoration one of these days. Then I painted the bedside trolley black with gold lining, and finally I have yielded to a sudden impulse to transform the overmantel mirror, perhaps because I find its prim Adam shape provoking. I have decided to give it a polychrome treatment. Most mornings I add another colour element, picking out a moulding, or glazing a red to a maroon, and almost every night I look at it critically and decide to change it all again. But that is the way decorative painting goes as soon as you break with tradition and try for something personal and different. There are few decorative painters I respect more than Graham Carr, and I have Graham's word for it that the only way to get something right is to be prepared to get it wrong, not just once or twice but for as long as it takes to attain that flow of certainty, the conviction that you have achieved the revised but definitive version. If John Fowler was prepared to paint a room out and start again, half-a-dozen times if necessary, in order to realize the vision in his mind's eye, why should we lesser visionaries be too proud?

A splendidly handsome rope border can be built up from three separate stencils, first the background, then the zig-zags in contrasting colours to suggest shading.

2

CREATING COLOURS

When colour is so sumptuous and pleasurable, as well as cheap and accessible, it puzzles me that so many people still approach colour in decorating with such misgivings. Instead of revelling in this inexpensive luxury and taking inspiration from all the colour expertise that surrounds us in shop windows, posters, magazines and clothes, they are paralysed by fears that colour is too hot to handle without professional training – as if it were necessary to be a chef to cook, or a Wine Master to appreciate a glass of claret. Although some people do seem to be born with an extra sensitivity to colour, just as others may have perfect pitch, colour sense, like any other sense, can be strengthened and sharpened simply by using it. Besides, you do not have to be a great, innovative colourist to put together attractive and successful decorating schemes.

One colour plus white is an easy formula which always looks effective, especially with a sophisticated colour like this pale terracotta. Note how it is carried over onto the ceiling. Cold and warm colours of similar value make restful painted stripes. This is one of the easiest finishes to do, thanks to masking tape.

To cultivate your colour sense you should begin by training yourself to *look*, with an assessing eye. When some colour effect attracts your attention, apple blossom maybe, or regimental uniforms, try to see it in relation to the other colours present. It is understanding how colours affect each other that makes for confidence in using them. It is not just the pink and white of the blossom to which your eye responds, but the blue of the sky, the sombre tone of the bark, the medley of greens in the leaves, even the tiny spark of yellow in the stamens. As Bauhaus colour theorist Josef Albers concluded: 'Colour is the most relative medium in art.'

To get an impression of the overall colouring of a scene rather than the detail, try half-closing your eyes until the subject is almost a blur. Taking in the colouring – which colours, in what proportions – is not much more complicated than figuring out what ingredients comprise the flavour of a particular dish. It soon becomes an automatic response, and it is this mental store of colour relationships that good colourists draw on all the time.

Subjective Colours

Everyone has a personal colour harmony, a combination of colours which they find most pleasing. Johannes Itten, another famous colour theorist, defined this personal selection as 'subjective colour' and he was emphatic that identifying and using our subjective colours does more than make our environment more attractive. 'To help a student discover his subjective forms and colours is to help him discover himself.'

That only sounds far-fetched if you have never progressed beyond the childhood idea of one 'favourite' colour. Even that can be a useful point of departure. If you are drawn to one colour, like red, in your clothes or furnishings, you inevitably begin seeing other colours in relation to red when you decide, for example, what coloured shoes to wear with a red dress. You will know, too, that there are many colours or tones which can be classified as 'red'. You may put two or three colours together with your red dress one day which make the dress sing out in a way it has not done before, and you have the indefinable feeling that something has clicked into place.

Using your subjective colours in your immediate surroundings is not just pleasurable, it is therapeutic, just as living among alien colours, or neutral chromatic tones, can be strangely depressing. Itten believed that 'colours are forces, radiant energies which affect us positively or negatively whether we are aware of it or not.' He carried out an experiment on some of his students in which they were kept first in a blue-green painted room, then in a room painted orange-red. They began to feel cold in the blue-green room when the temperature dropped to 59 degrees, while in the orange-red room they did not complain of the cold until the temperature had dropped a further 5 degrees, or in some cases 7 degrees. Orange-red is unconsciously perceived as the colour of warmth.

Colours do not have to be 'colourful' in the obvious sense – bright or strongly contrasting – to have an emotional effect or a psychological importance. Some people are drawn to muted, subdued shades, just as some painters like to work with a muted palette.

Rules and Theories

I never refer to colour systems, like colour wheels or charts, when I am thinking about the colours I might combine in a room. I do not know any decorators, or decorative painters, who do, though artists like Alan Cuthbert find a knowledge of colour theory and principles helpful as well as fascinating. What Alan Cuthbert does consciously, many other colour-minded people probably do unconsciously, registering impressions of interesting, subtle, or beautiful colour mixtures without stopping to analyse what made them memorable. Very often, when you do analyse a particularly successful colour combination it does in fact conform to established principles.

The study of colour is a complex science, but you will find it a great help when experimenting with paint colours if you are at least familiar with the basic rules and terms, however obvious. Colour begins, literally, with hue. The hue – red, blue, mauve – *is* the colour, the element that differentiates it from all others. The 'tone' or 'shade' of a colour refers to the degree of lightness or darkness. If the colour or hue is blue, for instance, the blue tones will be all those shades that result from adding increasing amounts of white, or lightness, or increasing amounts of black, or darkness, to the original pure blue. Pigment is the substance itself, the raw material of colour, which is sometimes derived from natural materials, sometimes from chemical processes. Many pigments have an undertone of another colour that is hard to identify. Two full-strength blues may look quite similar, but when you add white to both and compare the pastel shades, the different undertones show up clearly. The most useful way to classify colours for decorating purposes is to group them into 'warm' and 'cold' categories, but there are warmer versions of cold colours, and vice versa.

The Colour Tribe

Red, blue and yellow are the three primaries with which we are all familiar. Primary means first, or original, and the almost infinite number of colour permutations – around a million identifiable shades, according to Alan Cuthbert – all derive from this trio, plus black and white. Some decorative painters, and colour mixers like Cyril Wapshot, use only these five basic colours to make all the other colours that they need. In some ways this is a convenience – you need carry only five tubes of pigment around with you – but it can take longer to mix colours than would be the case with a wider range, and some painters feel it gives cruder, less controlled results. Secondary colours are produced by mixing two of the primaries (orange from yellow plus red, purple from red plus blue, green from blue plus yellow). But it is the tertiaries, made by mixing the primaries with secondaries (red plus orange giving orange-red, blue plus green giving blue-green), and the tones or shades obtained by lightening or darkening them, which really supply the sort of colours decorators use. The further a colour is from a primary, the less vivid it is and the easier to combine with other colours of the same intensity. Vivid hues are exciting, especially when used together, but generally they are too challenging to live with in any quantity. The tones or shades obtained by lightening, darkening or intermingling colours are much less visually demanding. It is these colours that decorators value most.

When the colours are arranged as they are on our artist's palette, another and very important relationship emerges – the complementaries. The colour opposite any given colour on the palette is its complementary – the complementary of the primary red is secondary green, that of tertiary blue-purple is tertiary orange-yellow.

Complementary colours balance each other visually. Physiologically, we seem to need this colour balance. This, at least, is one way of explaining why if you look hard at any colour for about twenty seconds and then look at a plain white or grey sheet of paper, the complementary colour immediately appears as an after-image. (See our colour boxes with grey centres on p. 32.) Grey works as well as white because it is chromatically neutral.

The arrangement of colours on our artist's palette demonstrates an important colour relationship. The colour opposite any given colour on the palette is its complementary – the complementary of the primary red is secondary green, the complementary of tertiary blue-purple is tertiary orange-yellow. A knowledge of complementary colours is invaluable when balancing a colour scheme.

For decorating purposes, the value of complementaries is in balancing a colour scheme. Just suppose that a room has become overwhelmed by, say, blue-purple. You could immediately rectify matters by introducing a flash of orange-yellow. This may sound crude as a decorating scheme, and in fact you would be more likely to use paler tones of purple like mauve or lavender (whose complementary would be a similarly lightened tone of orange-yellow), but it provides a useful pointer when hunting for the colour that will irradiate a scheme that feels unbalanced and lifeless. Not merely the direct complementary, but also colours adjacent to it on our artist's palette will marry happily – in the case of lavender, this will include all those colours from yellow-green to brown-red, or rather their paler versions – almond green and salmon pink.

Mixing equal amounts of complementary paint colours always gives grey. Mixing a little of one colour into a lot of its complementary has a softening effect, which is useful to know if you need to dull or soften a bright paint colour without altering its tone.

Colour Values

Talk of colour values sounds pretentious, but it helps to know what the term means because an understanding of colour values is important to the success of close combinations of colours, as in a stencilled pattern. If you have ever tried to work out sympathetic colours for a three-colour border, and found one colour 'jumped' out at you restlessly, it is because you got the colour values wrong. Value in this context means vividness or intensity, and the secret of a pattern or blend which 'lies flat' and knits together harmoniously is to use colours of similar value. The stripes which decorator Nemone Burgess painted on the walls of her bedroom are an example of colours which work together. They are restful rather

Primary colour on a white ground jumps out at you and looks strident over a large area. By bringing the colour values closer, darkening the background and softening the motif colour, the pattern 'lies flat'. Adding the complementary colour in more or less equal quantities has a similar balancing effect and enriches the pattern.

than restless stripes, because the colours used are of the same value. If either colour were a few degrees brighter, it would seem to be advancing while the other was receding, and this would be disturbing when repeated throughout the room.

One way of working out whether colours are of approximately the same value is by imagining them photographed in black and white. Colours of similar intensity will come out as similar tones of grey. If you stencilled red flowers on a white ground and photographed them, the flowers would be almost black in relation to the ground. Maximum contrast of this kind will always look 'jumpy' on walls, though a fabric designer might like the excitement that this creates. Wall patterns, even on the limited scale of a border, work best where no one colour predominates, so to make this idea work you would need to raise the ground colour value to, say, a warm buff colour, and 'knock back' the flowers. You could do this either by mixing the red with green or raw umber to give a softer red, or by framing the red flowers with green leaves, since red and green juxtaposed neutralize each other. This would also make a more satisfactory, richer looking pattern.

Another example comes from my own house. The mid-blue lines, painted to form a 'frame' for the pink walls of my sitting room, looked too hard and emphatic. The blue was too intense for the soft transparent background because these colours are of different tonal values. 'Dirtying' the blue with thin washes of raw umber, burnt umber and a little burnt sienna, rubbed on with a rag, unevenly for speed, produced a dull blue-green close to the colour of weathered copper. This was not only closer in value to the pink but, because of the green tone, was nearer to being the straight complementary of the pink, and as a result the walls and painted framework settled down harmoniously as if made for each other.

The Family of Tones

As you experiment with mixing colours you will find some that are immediately attractive, others that are odd but interesting and some that are frankly depressing or displeasing. Fortunately for those of us who need guiding through the colour jungle, this vast range of colours has been winnowed over the centuries by decorators, painters and other colour-minded people. It is not easy to define what makes a 'good' colour; most decorators have their own favourites (see pp. 34–5, 38), but they all recognize a good colour even if it lies outside their personal range of preferences, which suggests that 'good' is not a purely subjective judgement. Broadly, I would define a good colour as one interesting enough to look at in its own right, positive enough to allow other colours to be played off against it, but subdued enough to remain a background to furnishings, pictures, possessions and people.

Now and then, a good colour becomes a fashionable decorating trend, and you see it so often that it begins to look jaded. Apricot is an outstanding recent example, with terracotta, in its paler shades, a close second, and currently mauve is coming up strongly. But the caprices of fashion do not alter the fact that good colours are classic decorating colours, and for this reason anyone interested in developing their colour sense should study them and see how they perform. The easiest way to do this is to leaf through decorating magazines, noting which colours look most effective. Recently, I saw photographs of a house where the bedroom had been painted, unexpectedly, in a moody but wonderful violet-grey, mixed to match thunder-clouds seen over the moors outside. Relieved by vivid patchwork, shiny old wood, lots of pictures and personal treasures, this colour, which might not normally be thought of as a 'bedroom colour', had strength and character, and immediately

An optical reflex which suggests an unconscious need to find a balance in colours. If you stare hard at each coloured square in turn, the complementary colour will appear over the neutral grey centre.

joined my mental file of attractive colour possibilities.

Among the few colours which are 'good' just as they come are the earth colours – ochre, raw and burnt sienna, raw and burnt umber, Indian or Venetian red – which are always satisfying, especially for exteriors, though even then most painters would modify them a little. There are others: indigo is a particularly good blue, as is cerulean, and Naples yellow, lemon yellow and Paynes grey also fall into this category.

However, a 'good' decorating colour is usually one which has come about by mixing several colours in varying proportions. Often, though not always, it is called a 'dirty' colour, dirty here signifying approval, and denoting a softening and mellowing of the original hue which is close to the effect of time. Ambiguity of tone, I think, is a common feature of most good colours in decorating. Blues will have a brownish or greenish cast, greys a violet or pearly tinge, pinks a greyish-brown tone, while yellows may be greyish or pinkish. Just why this makes them more effective as decorating colours is a little mysterious, but to anyone sensitive to these nuances – and this is where a developed colour sense leads you – the difference between one of these complex colours and a simpler one is almost palpable.

This brings me smack into my next point, which is that if you care enough about 'good' colours to want them around you, you will almost always have to mix them yourself. The commercial paint ranges are short on good colours, except in the paler neutral shades. Decorative painters do use them, but mostly for convenience as a base on which to apply their transparent paint effects. Graham Carr, for instance, used a commercial red as a base for the obelisk bookcases in his open-plan room, knowing that he could mix up a colour in glaze which would combine with the red base to give just the effect he wanted. It would have wasted time, and used up a great deal of tinting colour, to mix up the red base, as is the case with any strong colour. Transparent paint, as we shall see, solves many problems.

Some specialist paint firms pride themselves on marketing good colours, others will match a colour swatch for you. If you despair of being able to mix colours successfully, this could be your answer. Nothing, however, gives the same flexibility as taking your courage in both hands, getting a selection of tinting colours, and mixing up your own. As we all know, there is many a slip between colour sample and painted room; if you mix you can correct the colour on the spot.

Beginners in colour-mixing, as in cookery, need recipes. Knowing that you are on the right colour path makes all the difference. It also means that you know what ingredients – that is, tinting colours – to stock up on. Decorating colour formulas are something of a trade secret, information painters prefer to keep to themselves. I am grateful for the generosity with which many of them have shared their favourite formulas.

FAIL-SAFE COLOUR SCHEMES

I know from experience that some people take to the notion of mixing their own colours and building up their own colour schemes with no difficulty at all. For those who are less confident, it can be reassuring to know that there are many reliable basic colour schemes for rooms which always look attractive, and are easy to live with. Once you have got the basics together, adding experimental touches becomes easy and fun.

Painters know about the chemistry, and performance of colour because this is their special field of study. Analysing the 'palette', how much of which colours are used by your own favourite artist, can give helpful pointers when choosing a colour scheme.

Neutral rooms

The best neutral room schemes are costly looking. Use stone colours – putty, beige, greys and buffs – ranging in tone from the interesting off-whites to slate-greys, tobacco-browns and sepia. All these colours blend together easily in a room, are undemanding background shades for pictures, flowers and furniture, and create a cool, calm effect. The main problem with neutrals is that they can look drab. The remedy is to concentrate on textures – rough like matting, stone and wood, shiny like marble, lacquer, silk and satin, or soft and furry like velvet. For contrasting colour, add shiny black, dull red, or a bunch of cushions in mauve, pink or greeny-yellow. The best colours in standard paint ranges are neutral shades.

Monochrome rooms

Taking a favourite colour, and working through tones of it for the wall colour, furnishings and fabrics in a room, can give a surprisingly rich effect. It is important to mix warm and cold tones to keep it lively, and some contrast of texture will help too. A subdued use of pattern will prevent monotony. This monochrome effect is a popular one right now, and designers like Tricia Guild use it as the basis of a 'co-ordinated' look. Rooms like these look good with walls given a decorative paint finish in two tones, for instance dragged in mid-blue over light blue or ragged in terracotta over palest pink. For contrast, try small doses of the complementary colour in its paler shades.

Greyed-pastel rooms

Colour theorists often suggest taking colour ideas from flowers, but I feel this is risky because a growing flower needs to be seen in relation to its foliage. Dried flower colours, on the other hand, are softened to the point where they harmonize beautifully to form what Graham Carr calls 'old, dirty colours'. If you want to use many colours in a room successfully, you could try sorting out a packet of pot-pourri into its basic colours and using these as a starting point. Greyed or dirty pastels consort very happily together, and create a pretty, nostalgic effect. Try to introduce a few darker tones for strength, like the maroon of dried red rose petals or wallflowers, or the room may become too prettified. The drab green of dried leaves is another obvious, and safe, contrast colour.

White-plus-one-colour rooms

This is hardly original but it always works and looks fresh and appealing. Except for a young girl's bedroom, I would steer clear of brilliant white with a pastel colour; interesting off-whites (see p. 35 for details of what the experts use) plus tones of one sophisticated colour such as pale blue, brick-pink or violet-grey, would look more elegant and grown-up. The disadvantage, of course, lies in keeping it reasonably clean. It is essentially a country cottage look.

GOOD COLOURS AND HOW TO USE THEM : WHAT THE EXPERTS SAY

Mark Hornak is the son of another well-known decorative painter, Jean Hornak. Despite having been to art school himself, he says roundly: 'I find art students can't mix colours; most of them have never heard of burnt umber. They don't seem to have been taught to appreciate the earth colours, all those subdued hues which look so wonderful in room schemes. If you ask them for a yellow, they will hand you a chrome yellow, something that hits you in the eye. They'd never think of using a subtle yellow, like raw sienna. I don't like the colours that come from aniline dyes, like the chromes or viridian green. I'd always mix a little burnt sienna into viridian to kill it slightly. If I wanted a brighter yellow, I'd probably mix ochre with lemon yellow, maybe a little raw sienna, too. Beginners should start with a limited range – your five basic colours will do – extending it gradually into the brighter colours.

'The colours that hover between warm and cold are the good colours for me. We've been using a dark, dark green on some furniture, which is like the dark green you get on French coffee cups, almost black in some lights. It is one of those colours that have such depth you never get to the bottom of them.

'One of the most useful decorating colours is a good off-white. You can't buy one ready-mixed. The John Fowler formula was black, lemon-yellow, raw umber and maybe a little raw sienna mixed into white. I might use black, plus raw and burnt umber with white. My wife, Rosie, sometimes paints a whole room in different shades of this off-white; it looks not boring but lively, creating its own light and shade.

'Of course, there are lots of ways of arriving at the same colour, or coming close to it. I might make up an apricot using Windsor red, burnt sienna, spectrum yellow, raw sienna and white. If I wanted a dirtier colour, I would add raw umber. But you could get a similar apricot using quite different colours. I like to add a little black to my greens and blues; it gives them character. Ivory black is better than lampblack because it is transparent. But of course the way to get real depth of colour is with glazes, one colour on top of another, like the Old Masters used to do. There's nothing to beat transparent colour. We usually use a glaze over white, or off-white, to get that effect of reflected light shining through, but if you scumble, using a paler glaze over a darker colour, you get some really intriguing effects.

'You must like the colour yourself, that's important. Also, when you are mixing colours you should never see them in isolation – a decorating colour doesn't mean anything on its own, but only in relation to everything else in the room.'

Graham Carr also had an art school training, but really began learning about colour while working for John Fowler, accompanying him around country houses and the National Trust's historic buildings. Almost any detail of a Carr interior provides instruction as to how you can make surfaces more interesting with paint.

'I'm a great mixer. The only colours I don't use are clear, clean colours – pastels. I like dirty colours; to live with colours I think they have to be dirty but that may be because I love colours to look old, as if they had always been there. I don't stick to a few basic colours – I like to have lots of different yellows and reds, for instance, and I mix them up to get what I want, rarely the same mixture twice running. I use oil colours rather than stainers because I don't think stainer colours are as pure. I try to stick to historically correct colours for old rooms. I use the same colours in modern rooms, adapting them to suit or mixing in something a bit surprising. It's a question of going with, rather than against, the building.

'A good colour should act as a background to a room. You need to study what light does to it, and what that colour does for the people who live with it. If I want cheering colours, I keep to hot oranges, yellows and reds, but of course I mix in lots of other colours to make them more interesting.

'For a good off-white, I'd mix raw umber and black into white to get a pale stone colour, which is what off-whites really are. For a good blue, I'd start with cobalt, add a little black and just a touch of scarlet lake to warm it. I don't like ochre, it's too dead and flat. I prefer raw sienna – it's got

The 'before' and 'after' pictures of our painted transformation scene. 'Before' is a typical no-colour room – neutral and lifeless. 'After' shows how much more complete the same place looks when surfaces have been brought to life with colour and texture: ragged walls, a limed fireplace and grained door, dragged woodwork, a combed floor and a frieze stencil, based on the classic Greek key design and using colours related to the room scheme.

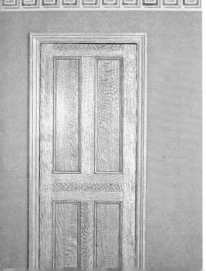

more life to it. For a yellow, I'd start with lemon-yellow, add raw sienna and a touch of vermilion. A good yellow should not be too green, or too hot. For a warm red, I'd probably use vermilion and scarlet lake for brightness, then burnt sienna and burnt umber to knock it back again.

'Transparent colour is what it's all about, really, because the great thing about transparent colour is that you can build it up to any shade you want. The red walls in a study I painted were coloured up with two shades of red glaze, one on top of the other, followed by a tinted varnish to give a real depth, like lacquer.'

Nemone Burgess has been a decorative painter for over twenty years, and taught herself by 'doing it'. She paints anything from chinoiserie-style patterns on walls to sky ceilings, or frivolous trompe l'œil shell decoration on a wooden lavatory seat. It is noteworthy that her colour range is rather different from the two male painters.

'I find myself using, and liking, a lot of mauve, aubergine, grey and yellow – a Chinese yellow, which is quite sharp. I have to say that I am personally bored with those canteloupe and peach colours that everyone loves at the moment, though of course I use them if that's what the client really wants. If I am working on something like a chinoiserie design I take my cue from the old hand-painted wallpapers and use all the colours of the rainbow. But for the usual paint finishes the following colours, in different combinations, are the ones I use most at the moment.

'If I were painting a mauve or aubergine finish, I might start with a grey or mauve undercoat which I would tint myself. I use stainers mostly for tinting; the stainer range has a wonderful Bordeaux purple which I use a lot and a violet which is good. I don't mix glazes to an exact formula; the amount of commercial glaze I use depends on the sort of finish I want. I use more when I need a ''globby'', stippled look, and less when I want the surface to be very flat and thin.

'To mix a grey I would use blue with a little black and maybe a dash of red oxide to enliven it. I tend to add a little black to any red colour I mix. My favourite earth colour is a terracotta. Terracotta has masses of blue in it, much more than anyone would think. I mix mine with blue, black, Bordeaux purple, and red oxide.

'Some painters always seem to go for strong, positive colours. I tend to stay with the wishy-washy ones, maybe because they are easier to live with and clients like them.'

TRANSPARENT PAINT: GLAZES AND WASHES

You will be aware by now that the paint used by the experts is unlike the commercial paints sold over the counter, which are fast-covering and therefore opaque. For convenience, it is often referred to as transparent paint as its translucent quality is immediately striking. Decorative painters use some commercial paints, but the 'special effects' which are their stock-in-trade are largely based on decorative manipulation of transparent paint to create effects which they could never achieve with the commercial panoply of gloss, semi-gloss or alkyd, matt or silk-finished emulsions.

Transparent paint has two outstanding properties. It allows colour to be introduced as a delicate film, so sheer that the colour beneath shines or 'grins' through. Over pale colours transparent paint adds colour with very little loss of luminosity, because light rays are reflected back from the base colour underneath. The delicacy and radiance of transparent colours used in this way are flattering to any room, particularly those problem rooms that are too dark or small. Alternatively, applying one colour over another, or perhaps three slightly differing tones of one colour on top of each other, you can build up colours that are richer, livelier and softer than any opaque paint could achieve. Transparent colour seems to dissolve surfaces and contours which is why it can do two apparently irreconcilable things: open out small spaces, and make large objects look less substantial.

The other property of transparent paint, which makes it the decorative painters' favourite medium, is that it takes impressions very readily. It can be patterned with rags, sponges and brush bristles to create complex textures unlike any others.

Given these attractions, it is hardly surprising that transparent paint and its uses became something of a trade secret. As soon as it was realized, however, that anyone could get hold of these materials and produce very creditable effects of their own without special training, decorative paint finishes became the new discovery in home decorating.

There are in fact several different forms of transparent colour in common use. In my experience, the type which is based on a proprietary transparent oil glaze is easiest to handle, and consequently the one that amateur decorators invariably settle for.

Glazes

Artists have used glazes since oil colour first became popular (Van Eyck is credited with the invention of oil painting) because transparent films of colour allow subtle effects in modelling, highlighting and building up flesh tints. An artist's glaze is usually composed of oil colour mixed with linseed oil and turpentine, or white spirit. The linseed oil adds strength and dries to a tough, durable film, while the solvent thins the mixture and speeds drying time. Decorative painters do make use of artists' glazes like these on occasion, but they usually add matt or eggshell varnish to the mixture to speed drying and give 'body' to what is otherwise a very fluid, fragile

mixture while wet. Len Pardon, whose virtuoso graining and marbling is shown in Chapter 3, often uses this type of glaze and his recipe is given in our Glaze Box.

Ready-made glazes, formulated specially for decorative painting over large areas like walls, are produced by specialist paint firms (see suppliers index). These come in varying consistencies but they all have substances like wax and drying agents added to make them hold decorative impressions clearly, dry faster (they are touch-dry within between four and eight hours as opposed to four days for the artists' mixture) and give a durable finish which does not need to be varnished for protection. However, most painters cover glazed walls with varnish just to be on the safe side.

Commercial glazes come uncoloured. In theory some can be used straight from the can with added tinting colour, but used in this way they dry to a rather thick, gummy texture which makes the decorative effects look coarse, 'like jam on bread' as Colefax-trained Susan Williams describes it. They are invariably used in a 'let down' form, thinned with white spirit. Enough commercial glaze should be used to hold marks clearly and encourage your mixture to stay wet, or 'open', for as long as possible, but not so much that it adds its own texture to the final finish. Relying on the commercial glaze to do the job for you is the mark of an amateur, but if you are inexperienced you will find a generous proportion of commercial glaze decidedly helpful. Start with the beginner's recipe in our Glaze Box, and progress to the more diluted recipes as you get more experienced.

Commercial glaze plus tinting colour plus white spirit gives completely transparent colour, which looks delicate and pretty in the paler pastel shades but can look 'jammy' when the colour is quite strong. Imagine a vivid coloured nail lacquer, and you will get the idea. Most pro-

Three swatches of the same colour showing the different effects of opaque paint, transparent glaze and a transparent wash.

fessionals, like Graham Carr and Nemone Burgess, add a varying amount of white undercoat or eggshell (mid-sheen) paint to their glaze mixture, at least one tablespoonful, to soften the colour slightly and make it a little cloudier.

How to mix a glaze

Use a white plastic paint kettle, because white shows up your glaze colour best, and a long-handled artists' brush with a good clump of firm bristles (a hogs'-hair brush, about 25 mm wide, would be fine) to keep your hands clean and disperse the colour effectively. Mix up tinting colours (artists' oil colour or commercial stainer colours – see suppliers index) separately in a white bowl, and use an old spoon to transfer colour to the kettle. Keep a few sheets of white paper handy for testing the colour (though you can use the wall itself if you rub the colour off again immediately with a rag dampened in white spirit); you will also find lots of old rags (old sheets are good for this) are invaluable.

Start by pouring commercial glaze plus white spirit into the kettle in the proportions given in the recipe you have chosen. Add the solvent to the glaze gradually, and stir with the brush to mix well. If you are using white undercoat or eggshell, mix it with the glaze before pouring in the white spirit. Half a litre of this mixture will be enough to glaze a small-to-average sized room, but it is better to make too much rather than too little. The extra glaze can always be kept in a screw-top jar for touching up purposes later on. Remember where possible to label the jar with the colour formula, because even a rough guide to the colours used is very helpful if you ever want to mix up that precise colour again. Another advantage of white paint kettles is that they come in standard sizes so you can estimate quantities at a glance.

It is impossible to be precise about the amount

This colour sample shows the different quality of transparent glaze with and without the addition of a white undercoat.

of pigment or stainer you will need, but if in doubt, use small quantities. Put a good squeeze of the main tinting colour into your bowl, then add proportionately smaller amounts of the other colours. Tip in a little of your mixed-up glaze base, stir very thoroughly with the long-handled brush, and then try a brushstroke on the white paper. Almost certainly it will be too light. Go on adding more of the prepared glaze mixture from the kettle, stirring each time and testing, until you have attained the right intensity. You may find this happens before you have used up the prepared glaze mixture, in which case you will need more colour, but scaled down to the quantity of glaze left. If you have used up all the glaze and it is still too light, add more of the glaze mixture, mixed up separately as before. You may be lucky and hit the shade you want quickly, but more often than not you will have to spend an hour or so getting it exactly right. Professionals expect to put time into this stage of the game, so do not be discouraged.

If you have mixed up a colour and do not feel quite happy with it, brush the colour thinly over a sheet of paper and let it dry. Glaze colours tend to settle down as they dry, and a larger expanse once dried will look softer than a small brushstroke when wet. If it is too dark, add more of the basic glaze mixture. If it is the right intensity but too vivid, add some of the complementary colour, first diluted in white spirit. If it needs to be toned down still further, try adding some raw umber which softens and mellows any colour, ageing it instantly. If, however, this is not the effect you want, and a clear shade is required, you have the choice of either lightening and softening it with white, which will take it towards a pastel colour, or shading it with black or one of the in-between greys, which will 'kill it' a little. Take Mark Hornak's tip and use transparent ivory black, but go slowly because a little can make a great difference to the more transparent pigments.

Colour on colour – variations on the glaze theme

In most cases professionals glaze with a pale colour over a white base. 'It's so much easier to ask the painters to do it all white,' Nemone Burgess explains. And white, with its reflectiveness, is often the best base colour for many glaze effects. But one variation, which is popular because it makes for a very rich tone of any given colour, is the use of a pastel or mid-tone colour for the base coat, which is then glazed over in a darker tone. It does not matter if the base colour is slightly out – too cold or too dull – because the glaze can be mixed to correct this. Mark Hornak's pyjama-stripe dragging (see p. 53) shows the difference between blue glaze over white and blue glaze over pale blue.

Amateurs could steal a march on the professionals, I feel, by trying out different colours on top of each other, burnt sienna over green, for instance, or lilac over grey or beige. The most

This is the sort of kit a decorative painter might carry about – artists' colours, specialist brushes, graining combs, glaze, a steel rule, sponge, scalpel, varnish and gold size. For amateurs, small is sensible to begin with. Note the curious graining gadget on the right for making knots and heartwood markings.

extraordinary, subtle colours can be arrived at in this way, as you can prove by experimenting on coloured boards.

One subtlety Nemone Burgess uses regularly consists of brushing a milky glaze over a terracotta base to reproduce the fine bloom you see on unglazed flowerpots. Paler glazes over dark colours can create attractive opalescent effects, and can also be a godsend if your wall colour turns out to be too bright. Brushing a pale glaze over the top is the quickest way to 'knock it back'.

Washes

Washes are another form of transparent paint used in decorative painting. They are soluble in water. There are various forms of water-based paint, but in practice decorators usually prefer gouache, acrylic colours, old-fashioned distemper (if available) or thinned-down standard flat emulsions, all 'washy' when thinned.

Colour diluted in water and thinly applied is called a wash. It is just as transparent as oil glaze but it has a freshness and purity which colours in oil cannot match, since the oil itself has a yellowing effect. Also, it dries to a matt, powdery, fragile finish, which is appealing, like a fine cotton lawn as opposed to a fine silk gauze. Colours which might look too rich when applied as a glaze look excellent in a wash. The difference is not striking, but it is noticeable. The warm earthy colours on my landing are painted with gouache sealed with matt varnish, and I think they have a better, drier texture than if they had been coloured with a glaze which would have fattened them up to something more like chocolate and toffee. The two problems with a wash colour finish are firstly that it is trickier to apply, since what we are talking about is virtually coloured water, and secondly even when sealed with varnish it is less durable.

The medium used most often for colour-washing walls is gouache colour, most intense of the water-based colours. When distemper paint

A good example of how colour which would blaze in an opaque paint becomes soft and glowing when ragged with transparent glaze over a white base. A shiny varnish adds sparkle and protection.

RIGHT *A demonstration in the use of complementary colours to balance a colour scheme. The vivid mauve of the walls could have been overwhelming without the accents of its complementary colour, yellow, but together they are a sophisticated combination.*

was commonly available it was popular with decorators like John Fowler for colourwashing because it contains enough whiting, or powdered chalk, to give a delicious powdery texture when dry. He used it thinned with water to create surfaces of rustic spontaneity and charm, the 'old cottage wall' look. Gouache, applied over a base of matt emulsion or vinyl, gives a similar texture, though it is less powdery.

Thinned flat emulsion used on its own has something of the wash quality, but the colour is never as luminous because of the 'plastic' content of modern convenience paints. Poster colours are also used by some painters, but mainly for graining and marbling. Another water-based paint which is used a great deal is acrylic colour, which dries almost immediately and can be overpainted without dissolving, but it would be expensive used over a large surface. Acrylics are used for stencilling as a rule, where their drying speed is a great advantage.

Applying a wash

The texture of the base coat of a wash finish is important – watery colour will not adhere readily to a smooth silky base, though the addition of a little Unibond or Copydex adhesive, or even a squeeze of washing-up liquid, can help. It is best to start with a surface as close as possible to the quality of blotting paper. Standard matt emulsion undercoat or acrylic primer is sold through builders' merchants and some DIY stores, and dries to a gritty finish, which may need smoothing off with sandpaper.

You will need a large soft brush, like those sold for pasting wallpaper, to apply the wash colour, and a second soft-bristled brush like a painter's dust brush (see suppliers index) for picking up trickles and drips, and for 'softening' streaks and over emphatic brushmarks. Spread plastic sheets or newspaper over carpets if they come close to the wall to prevent spatters. Keep some soft rags handy for mopping up trickles on paintwork. Clear matt varnish is best for sealing a watercolour finish and most painters prefer the least yellow product (see suppliers index). Use a separate brush for applying varnish. A white plastic paint kettle is again useful for mixing up the wash.

To mix up the wash colour put a good squeeze of gouache into your kettle, plus a tablespoonful of standard white emulsion to give it body. Add water gradually, mixing it very thoroughly indeed because a streak of undissolved watercolour makes a very big mark on a wall. Test the wash on white paper. When the colour is right, try the wash on the wall (you can always wipe it off again with wet rags). It will almost certainly start trickling down, but try catching the trickles with your dust brush and smoothing them into the coloured area. You need to move fast, using your brushes lightly, to achieve a softened effect. If the wash still seems to be streaming off, try adding a spoonful of Unibond adhesive, but no more than one level tablespoon per half litre.

For maximum colour variation and a 'dappled' effect, some painters like to apply wash colours in two successive coats. The first coat of colour is applied loosely over a white ground, covering the surface unevenly so that the colour build-up is intense in some spots, yet next to nothing in others. When this coat is perfectly dry, a second coat of colour is brushed on top, again loosely and unevenly. Streaks and splodges should be smoothed into the base colour with the softening brush. This finish suits pale, glowing colours best – all the dull pinks and warm yellows through to apricot and cantelope.

A second wash coat needs to be sensitively applied so as not to shift the first. An isolating coat of matt varnish can help here. All water-based wall finishes should be given a final coat of matt varnish to protect them.

Glaze Box

Beginners' glaze recipe

50% commercial oil glaze
50% white spirit
tinting colour
1 tablespoon of white oil-based paint, like
undercoat or eggshell, can be added per $\frac{1}{2}$ litre to
soften the hard-edged effect.

Standard glaze recipe

25% commercial oil glaze
75% white spirit
tinting colour
1 tablespoon undercoat or eggshell white paint per
$\frac{1}{2}$ litre.

Len Pardon's all-purpose glaze recipe

1 part raw linseed oil (slows drying but makes for
a harder finish when dry)
1 part white spirit
1 part clear matt varnish
For a softer effect, add up to 1 part white undercoat.

Mark Hornak's standard glaze mixture

1–2 parts white undercoat (depending on how
much opacity or transparency is required)
1 part commercial oil glaze
1 part white spirit
2 tablespoons raw linseed oil
artists' oils for tinting.

Graham Carr's glaze

Graham Carr frequently uses a glaze made up with
no transparent paint at all. His work for the
National Trust taught him to steer clear of
anything containing linseed oil, which has a
yellowing effect on colours in time. His thinned
undercoat glaze will not discolour but takes some
practice to handle as it 'goes off' much more
quickly. Depending on how much opacity he wants
from the glaze colour, which in turn depends on the
finish and the colours he has in mind, Graham uses
between 10% and 30% standard white undercoat,
making up the rest with white spirit and using
artists' oils to arrive at the colour he wants. A glaze
of this sort is not transparent like commercial
glazes, but any colour underneath shows through
slightly and a distressed finish will of course
reveal more.

3

PAINTING THE WALLS I

M A S T E R I N G   T E X T U R E

Although transparent paint is, in itself, attractive as a wall finish, its true appeal lies in the way it can be manipulated while wet to create a wonderful variety of effects. These subtle textures, suggestive of natural substances like stone, marble, foliage and feathers, seemed to be just what everyone was looking for five years ago or so. They were disenchanted with the dead 'plastic' surface and unmysterious colours of commercial paints, and although wallpaper offered an alternative, it seemed to be restricted to sub-William Morris florals and calico sprigs. It was inevitable that the more adventurous DIY spirits should cast about for something new, which would allow more control over the end results. Instead of frightening off the inexperienced, the challenge of experimenting with unfamiliar techniques has encouraged a newly independent approach. People are not afraid to take chances and make mistakes if they think they may end up with the house they have always envisaged.

A coarse stippled effect gives walls a texture almost like hessian, while lively under-the-brush work with dragging below the dado rail provides a handsome background to pictures and knick-knacks.

I see this refusal to be satisfied with other people's colours and designs as a minor but significant aesthetic revolution, and a healthy reaction against those 'off-the-peg' designs shown in glossy house-style catalogues. With a little perseverance you can find not only the right colour, but the precise shade you have in mind. You can go on to create as much or as little texture and pattern on your walls as you like, from a diaphanous veil of watercolour to the richest of stippled glazes covered with tinted varnish, giving you what Mark Hornak calls 'a colour you can fall into'.

I have included only one finish in this book which is technically demanding: the gesso and dry colour 'antiqued' finish invented by Jim Smart. Although impractical for most households, some of you may like to try it as it is very distinguished. Otherwise most of these decorative finishes are encouragingly straightforward, although they are usually best tackled by two people working in tandem unless you are very experienced, or the wall surfaces are small. Practise on a board until you are familiar with the one you have chosen and then launch off on the window wall. Imperfections are least visible here, and windows also provide a handy natural break in the strenuous business of applying the glaze and texturing it before it dries or 'goes off'.

Preparation

Preparing a room for decorating simply takes time and patience. All painters have yarns about walls which were filled and rubbed down time and again until the surface was flawless and as flat as plate glass. Of course such perfectionism is unrealistic, but high standards of preparation do show in the end. Those professionals who bother most about details also tend to be the most deft, expert and successful. You must therefore balance the satisfaction of working on clean, smooth surfaces against how much time you can spare and how long you need your decorating to last.

Minimum preparation requires the following: all surfaces must be dusted and washed down with a weak solution of a grease-cutting cleaner like sugar soap (tops of doors and window-frames need special attention as grime and dust accumulate here); cracks, holes and chips in the plaster should be filled with standard or fine surface filler, sanded back until smooth and level when dry, and touched in with undercoat or base coat to seal it before painting; one, or preferably two coats of base paint, lightly rubbed down when dry with medium or fine grade sandpaper to remove grit, hairs and trickles, and then quickly brushed over with a dust brush. The ideal base paint for most finishes is an old-fashioned, oil-based eggshell, or mid-sheen paint, as this is smooth and non-absorbent. It is, however, a slow, heavy paint to brush out evenly and many people find that a silk vinyl emulsion, which has similar qualities, is easier to handle.

The commonest mistakes amateurs make are not sealing in the filler adequately (which leaves streaks of colour in your glaze finish because it is so much more absorbent) and not bothering to rub the walls down after applying the base coats. It is surprising how much dust settles on paint as it dries. If you are worried about cutting through the base paint at this stage – which can easily happen with vinyls – use a fine grade wet-and-dry paper and very light pressure.

However carefully you go, some glaze always smudges onto the ceiling or cornice and over the adjacent woodwork. Do not try to avoid this as it will inhibit your style. You can touch the smudges out later, or, if you are redecorating the whole room, you should paint the ceiling first (any subsequent smudges can be touched out) but leave the woodwork at the primer stage until you have finished. While the glaze is still wet, it can be easily rubbed off woodwork with a rag dampened with white spirit, but be careful not to smudge your wall finish.

Tools and Materials

These are the basic tools that you will need – the special tools for specific finishes are listed in the practical sections that follow.

Good quality housepainters' or DIY brushes should be used for applying base paint and glaze. A 75 mm brush is a good all-purpose size, but you will find a wider one helpful when applying glaze (this should be kept separate). Use a special varnishing brush for applying final varnish and clean it well with white spirit, then soapy water. For mixing colours a smaller brush is useful, a standard 12 mm painters' brush at a pinch, but preferably a firm bristled artists' brush with a long handle. Two or three of these will save time in cleaning, as you will need a clean brush each time you experiment with a new colour. It is good practice to knock a brush hard against something solid before use, just to shake off the clinging debris of old paint. I sometimes rake them through with a wire brush if they look clogged.

White plastic paint kettles are cheap, light and handy. White sets off your own colour well, and they come with lids to keep glazes and other preparations overnight.

Your step-ladder should be light, strong and aluminium for manoeuvrability and safety.

Buy a large keg of white spirit, at least 1 litre. Nothing is more exasperating than running out of this essential solvent.

For mixing colours I often use small foil containers sold for freezers, which can be thrown away after use; otherwise, use saucers or bowls. Keep a box full of empty jamjars with lids for odd mixing purposes – you can never have enough. A couple of old metal spoons are useful for adding small quantities of this and that.

You will need a large supply of old rags for mopping and cleaning up, best made from torn-up, worn-out old sheets, and plenty of waste-paper – old newspapers or lining paper is fine – for testing colours and brushing out remaining paint and glaze before cleaning your brushes.

Tints

Tinting colour comes in various forms and any specific requirements are listed separately with the instructions for the finish. Professionals tend to use artists' oil colours for tinting because the colours are more finely differentiated and stable, but universal stainers, available in tubes in most DIY shops, have the advantage that they can be used for tinting both oil- and water-based paints. The range of colours available is always improving. They are also very intense and are economical to use.

Glazes

Ratcliffes, Craig and Rose, and Bolloms all produce a basic glaze preparation to which you add colour and solvent. Bolloms's glaze is the thickest in texture and most prone to yellowing, while the Craig and Rose Luxine Glaze is generally considered the most delicate (which can make it harder to control) and least likely to yellow with time. A 1-litre can of any of these will go a long way – enough to cover two or more average size rooms, depending on the glaze recipe (see p. 47).

OVERLEAF

1 *Ragging in a subdued blue (ultramarine, indigo, a little of both umbers, a speck of black) over off-white gives an elegant crushed velvet texture.*

2 *Starting with two tones of green, warm over cold, Mark Hornak spattered on off-white, brown-black and golden yellow to create an old endpapers look.*

3 *This example of sponged-on colour uses five contrasting colours, but because they balance each other visually, the effect is not overpowering.*

4 *Rag-rolling in spaced out stripes over gentle ragging in a sharp, rich yellow gives a dramatic moiré effect.*

5 *Mark's dragging, done with a chopped-away brush. Note the different results when the thundery blue is dragged over white, and then over pale blue.*

6 *An under-the-brush finish creates spontaneous, 'painterly' effects, best in good colours like this mellow red.*

1

2

3

4

5

6

RAGGING

Ragged effects are achieved by pressing soft bundled-up rags into wet glaze in a constantly changing direction to make a flowing pattern with the look of damask or brocade. It can be played down until it is simply texture – I have seen rooms in which a creamy glaze was ragged over off-white to look like parchment – or stepped up dramatically using contrasting colours or two layers of slightly different coloured glazes. Nowadays, the favourite colouring is a soft apricot glaze over off-white. This is warm and pretty but needs some colour contrast.

Materials

For soft lint-free rags you can use old torn-up sheets, or industrial cloth, which is particularly favoured by painters for its crisp prints and absence of fluff. For different effects there is a whole variety of materials that you can try for added texture, such as well-washed hessian, crumpled plastic bags, paper or chamois leather.

Method

This finish is easier with two people. Starting in one corner, the first person brushes on a strip of glaze, about 30 cm wide, or whatever seems manageable, from top to bottom. The glaze need not be brushed out absolutely smoothly, but it should cover the base coat and be sufficiently even to allow the ragged prints to register clearly. When the glazer gets half way down the wall, the second person hops up the ladder and begins ragging into the wet glaze. The rag should be bunched up in one hand, tight enough to make a controllable wodge, but loose enough to give a busily folded pad – it is the folds that print the patterning. Simply press the pad into the glaze, changing the direction of your hand all the time and covering the area of wet glaze. While the second painter is ragging from the middle to the bottom of the wall, the first painter should be up the ladder brushing glaze onto the next strip. The strips should overlap just a little, but not so heavily that the glaze colour builds up as a stripe.

You will rapidly discover how much pressure to put on the pad in order to obtain distinct but not heavy-handed impressions and a soft flow of colour. Stand back from time to time to check that your work is fairly even – it will look more even as it dries. 'Skips', where the glaze is thin or the ragging indistinct, can be touched in lightly with the glaze-wet rag. Areas where the glaze has built up are best rubbed off carefully with a rag dampened with solvent, and then glazed and ragged over again, feathering in where the new glaze hits the first glaze coat. As a rule, however, the minute you hang pictures and replace the furniture, small unevennesses recede and become unnoticeable.

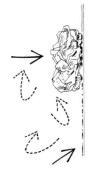

Ragging prints the marks of crumpled fabrics into wet glaze. Use a variety of fabrics for different effects – chamois leather, cheesecloth, gauze, industrial cloth, well-washed cotton and linen. As cloths become saturated with glaze, they should be replaced. Folds need rearranging frequently, too, to avoid repetition. Change the direction of the prints continually when ragging to avoid monotony.

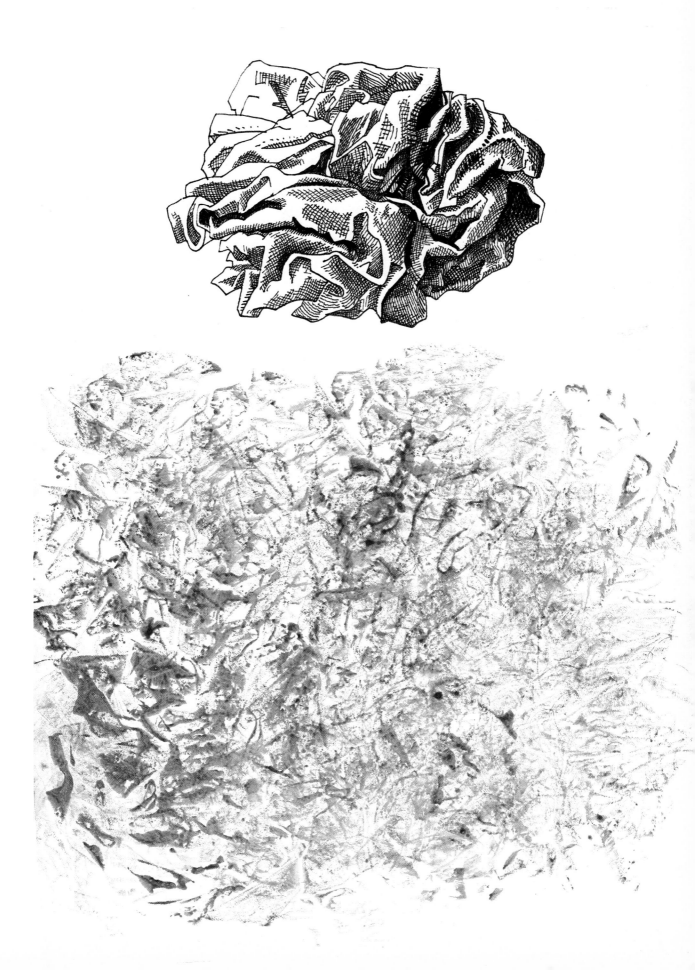

ABOVE LEFT *A lot going on here in the 'special effects' line – two kinds of marbling, fake panels in two tones of sharp yellow, coarsely dragged over white inside the panels and more finely dragged over yellow for the surrounds. The panels are further indicated by painted outlines in shades of grey.*

LEFT *A close-up of the same walls showing the vigorous brushiness of a dragged finish, and also how it consorts urbanely with an elegantly mounted and framed drawing.*

ABOVE *The remarkable yellow associated with Colefax and Fowler owes its depth and vibrancy to at least three coats of differently toned yellow glazes applied over a standard margarine-yellow base. Two coats of tinted varnish bring it up to a lacquer brilliance.*

RAG-ROLLING

Method

The same *modus operandi* applies, but here the rags are bunched into a shape like that of a small muff, and rolled up the wet glaze from bottom to top with the merest overlap where one roll-up meets the next. This effect looks more directional, almost stripey but not quite, because the surface of the roll changes in use. In all ragging processes the rags themselves will need changing occasionally as they become clogged with glaze. You should either re-bunch, or swap them for a new supply.

RAGGING PLUS ROLLING

Mark Hornak used a vivid yellow to demonstrate this one for us (see p. 53 for colour illustration, and p. 47 for the Hornak glaze recipe).

Method

For this finish, which is again best done by two people, a strip of wet glaze is first ragged lightly and quickly with scrumpled kitchen paper or tissue paper, just enough to give it a mottled look. Then, using a roll of soft muslin bunched into a little bolster about 20 cm long, roll a stripe up the mottled and still-wet glaze to create a rather formal, moiré effect. Then move onto the next strip of wet glaze, mottling and then rolling another stripe about 13 cm away from the first. The chief problem with this highly decorative finish is keeping the verticals lined up. Mark Hornak suggests pencilling guidelines on the wall before glazing, using an HB pencil which will not show under the glaze finish.

DRAGGING

This is less popular than ragging because it is hard to get slick vertical pin-stripes without a great deal of practice, but it looks crisp and elegant, especially in eighteenth-century rooms. The character of dragging changes with the type of brush used, since the finish consists of deliberate brushmarks made by dragging bristles through wet glaze.

Materials

To get a very fine striping, use a fairly wide fine-bristled brush, such as a varnish or paper-hangers' brush. Worn-down bristles will give rougher, less regular stripes which some people prefer.

Method

As with all glaze work, it is important to keep a speedy rhythm going, one person laying on the glaze, the other dragging, to prevent the glaze hardening or 'going off'. If the glaze is applied in narrow strips, and includes a fair amount of commercial oil glaze, this problem should not occur. If it does, the solution is to rub off the dry patch and re-glaze. A good rule to remember is do not stop until you reach a corner, which gives a natural break.

Dragging a high wall is usually done in two movements, from the top down as far as you can reach, then from the bottom to meet the top section, feathering off the meeting point to blend the dragged stripes together. It is almost impossible for amateurs to avoid a slight build-up of colour at the top and bottom of each dragged strip where your brush pressure changes slightly. Wiping the brush clean on a rag and very gently re-brushing over these areas can help to even out the colour, but it must be done straight away

In rag-rolling, a sausage of rags is rolled up or down wet glaze to create a directional effect, which is more forceful than simple ragging. Mark Hornak combines the two for interest (see p. 53).

before the glaze 'goes off'. If you find it difficult to keep a steady vertical brushstroke going while descending a ladder, you have one explanation for why most decorative painters prefer to keep dragging as a finish for woodwork, where surfaces are altogether smaller and more controllable.

MARK HORNAK'S DRAGGING FINISH

Mark Hornak's father used to lament the good old days 'when dragging was so much more virile'. This dashing effect is Mark's attempt to put back some of its lost vitality.

Materials

To get bold stripes, Mark chopped a whole row of bristles off a paper-hangers' brush, leaving a much thinned but even row of bristles. Thin bristles clump together when you brush paint on with them. But to make the stripes still heavier he went a step further. The glaze was poured onto an enamel plate with a slightly convex bottom to it, so that as he drew the brush through the glaze it picked up more colour on the outer bristles and less in the middle. Hence the 'thick, thin, thick, thin' effect across the wall.

Colourways

To soften the bold striping a little, it was painted tone on tone – a moody blue over a pale blue background. The background colour was made by tinting white eggshell (or vinyl silk) with permanent blue, ultramarine and a little raw umber to give a warm light blue, like a sunny day. Mark used artists' colours for tinting the oil-based eggshell – but remember to use a colour that dissolves in water if painting with a water-based vinyl.

FAKE LACQUER

Stippling is often used by painters to build up a fake lacquer effect. The deep glowing colour and smooth shiny surface looks chic and dramatic, especially at night, reflecting back lamplight.

Preparation

A very high standard of preparation is needed for this finish to look good, as grit, dust and other flaws really stand out on a high-shine surface. The painters I have talked to all have their own ways of achieving this particular finish. The most elaborate method uses differing tones of water-colour with a sealing coat of matt 'guard', or wallpaper seal, in between each wash, finishing with two coats of tinted varnish, stippled on. This gives extraordinary depth of transparent colour, but 'took for ever', according to decorative painter Carolyn Benson.

Fake lacquer can, however, be done more simply. The colour needs to be extra transparent, so the glaze mixture should have very little white undercoat added to it. A little clear matt varnish in the glaze will help counteract the thickness of the commercial glaze preparation. Two or three layers of glaze are applied in the usual way, each tinted to a slightly different tone. A blue-red glaze over a warmer orange or brown-red glaze looks richer and more interesting than if one glaze is mixed up to combine all these tones. Take great care to brush on the glaze smoothly, then stipple it closely with a soft brush to even out the colour and eliminate any brushmarks. All brushes need extra careful cleaning between sessions. A professional stippling brush, made of badger hair, comes into its own for fake lacquering as it has a comparatively large bristle surface. Unfortunately, these brushes are so expensive that many painters make do with what they can find in the

PREVIOUS PAGES Stippling is a simple way of giving an almost imperceptible, suede-like bloom to any tinted glaze colour, like the acid yellow carried over all the surfaces shown here.

Perfect dragging is difficult to achieve on large surfaces like walls, but makes an interesting surface on woodwork and furniture. Many professionals use worn-out standard brushes rather than a dragging brush, as shown here, for built-in variety.

LEFT *An under-the-brush finish in a 'dirtied' soft blue gives just enough wall texture to carry the bravura bedhead treatment of stripes, frills and gilt corona.*

ABOVE *Carried over the cupboard wall in a large 'panel' which ignores the placing of doors, the lively finish 'fades out' a lot of boring joinery.*

BELOW *A close-up of the brushy finish, applied over a white base after the surround has been masked off. When the glaze dries, the tape is peeled off, leaving neat edges.*

way of a soft flat-bristled brush – clothes brushes, shoe brushes or painters' dust brushes, for example. You should allow sufficient time between applying glaze coats for the previous coat to dry hard – preferably overnight.

The final varnish is vital to the lacquer look and it must be applied smoothly and evenly, with as few brushmarks as possible. There should be no 'skips' or bare patches. The varnisher should avoid going back over the same patch too often because the uneven build-up of varnish creates slight variations of colour as well as texture, at least on walls at right angles to the light source. Apply one or even two coats of shiny varnish – this can also be tinted if further modification to the colour is needed after glazing. Some painters use standard gloss varnish, slightly thinned down or mixed with eggshell polyurethane, while others go for the 'high deep gloss' of old-fashioned carriage varnish.

STIPPLING

Method

This is a straightforward finish to apply, feasible for one person working alone – if you are strong and speedy. Wet glaze is brushed on a strip at a time, and then distressed with the tip of a soft-bristled brush. Stab the bristles gently into the glaze to break up the colour into a myriad of dots. It is a useful way of softening any rich, strong colour to give a suede-like texture. It also breaks up the 'gummy' look of undoctored commercial glaze.

Try applying a richly-coloured glaze over a base colour just a couple of tones paler. The texture is not pronounced, but you have only to compare a stippled and unstippled patch to see how a broken surface glaze enriches and softens the whole effect.

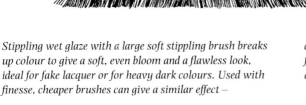

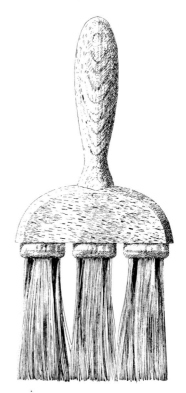

Stippling wet glaze with a large soft stippling brush breaks up colour to give a soft, even bloom and a flawless look, ideal for fake lacquer or for heavy dark colours. Used with finesse, cheaper brushes can give a similar effect –

a dust brush or shoe brush as shown above would be a fraction of the price. Apply with even pressure at right angles to the wall surface.

MARBLING

Marbling in paint can be done on any surface providing it has been properly prepared, which means primed, filled, undercoated, fine-filled, and then given two coats of eggshell. Whatever you do, don't do any filling in the eggshelled surface or the colour will soak in and leave a mark in your marble.

Materials

Len Pardon, a maestro of marbling, uses what he calls basic glaze for marbling. This is made with equal parts of raw linseed oil, white spirit (not turps substitute which is less refined) and ordinary white undercoat. In a room where the air is moving this will dry in twenty-four hours, and I mean twenty-four hours, not overnight. A fan heater gives the right air movement. If you need to dry it faster, or if the room is damp, the addition of some matt varnish in proportions of roughly 1 breakfast cup to 2½ litres of glaze will speed drying time.

Len always uses regular artists' oil colours to colour the glaze and to paint with, rather than universal stainers whose colour is less permanent. The brushes you will need are: a white hogs'-hair filbert (size 30) for applying oil colour, a lining fitch for taking colour off, and a Whistler Lilyduster which has tapered bristles for softening. You will also need a goose feather, a soft white rag and white spirit.

Method

Countless varieties of marble are quarried in the hills of Siena in Italy. *Broccatella* is Len's favourite.

The colours most commonly found in marble from this area are raw sienna, yellow ochre, burnt umber, ivory black, burnt sienna and a little blue. For *broccatella*, use raw sienna, ochre, burnt umber and ivory black. The glaze consists of 1 part each of white spirit, white undercoat and raw linseed oil, well mixed.

1) Brush the glaze on evenly. With a white hogs'-hair filbert (No 30) and a squeeze of raw sienna, form a strata in the glaze, adding yellow ochre over and around the sienna, as shown.

2) Immediately after this stage, dip the brush tip into burnt umber, then into black, and paint in angular veinings, together with crossed veins.

3) Rag the whole surface lightly with a crumpled cotton rag.

4) With a badger softener, or dust brush, soften the whole surface by holding the bristles at right angles to the surface and brushing gently in all directions to create a suffused, opaque finish.

5) With the tip of a goose feather dipped first in white spirit, then in ivory black, go lightly over the veins with colour to accentuate their depth. Then, using white spirit only, put in the fine crystalline fractures. Finally, soften again.

Professional marblers use a goose feather to put in veining because it breaks up the colour naturalistically. Hold the goosefeather loosely, like a diviner's rod.

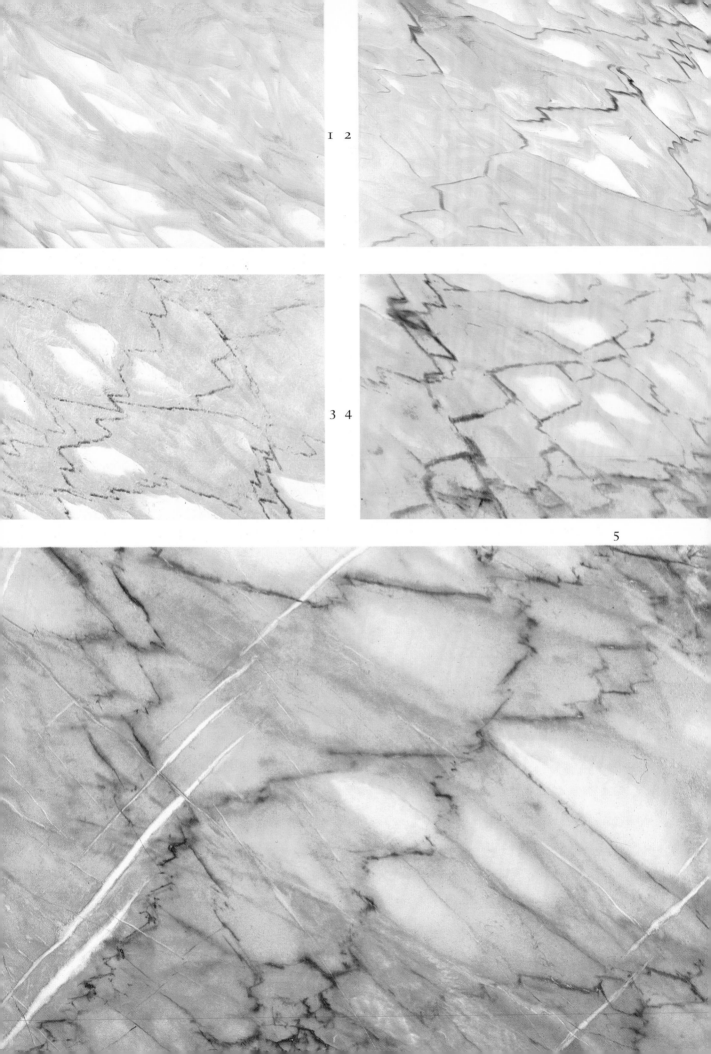

1 2

3 4

5

SPATTERING

Wonderfully complex colour effects can be built up on any surface by spattering – or raining dots of different coloured paints over a coloured or neutral base. Spattering is easy enough to do, but requires a certain judgement as to which colours to combine, and how heavily to spatter them. It also makes a lot of mess, as some flicked colour always ends up where it is not wanted. A room which is to be spattered needs to have everything masked off but the walls, unless the rest of it is to be painted over later. The trade usually keeps spattering for furniture and fireplaces for this reason, but it can make a spectacular wall finish.

Materials

Flat emulsion, tinted with stainers or gouache colours, is a good medium to use as its opacity helps the tiny spots to stand out instead of blending in as they tend to do with a transparent paint.

Method

The simplest spatter finish is done by flicking two or three colours onto a plain flat emulsion base in a suitably neutral shade. A safe guide when assembling colours is to stay within tones of one colour, but add some off-white for lightening and blending, and a very fine spatter of near-black (or the darkest tone of the predominant colour) to sharpen it all up at the end. Speckled stone colours are particularly effective.

Thin the emulsion with water – but not too much. Test the consistency by flicking against the wall experimentally (it can be wiped off again with a wet sponge). The spots should be quite fine and should stay put without turning into blots or trickling off. If they all start running, add more emulsion.

When spattering large areas, like walls, painters use a standard decorating brush, 50–75 mm in size, which they dip in the paint and then rap sharply against a piece of wood held in the other hand, so that spots of paint rain onto the nearest surface. This is a quick way of spattering large surfaces, but it needs rehearsing first on lining paper or a spare wall to get the knack of it. How far you stand from the wall, how hard you knock the brush, how much paint you take up on the brush – all these factors affect the result.

For closer control, usually over small areas, you can spatter effectively using a short stiff brush like a stencil brush, flicking your forefinger upwards over the bristles in a quick staccato movement. This gives finer spatters which can be aimed very precisely, but you need to stand closer to the surface itself.

 MARK HORNAK'S SPATTER FINISH

This is a de-luxe version of spattering, aiming at the depth of colour of fine old marbled endpapers. A cool blue-green base of tinted eggshell was first lightly ragged with a transparent glaze in a darker, yellower green. Crumpled paper was used to mottle the wet glaze. First, an off-white (almost a cream, as pure white on green looks blue) was used, then a bitter chocolate brown-black, and finally a light, uneven spatter of golden yellow made with a higher proportion than usual of ochre gouache to white emulsion (see p. 52).

A light freckling of shiny gold looks rich on some spattered finishes. This can be achieved by mixing bronze powder (obtainable from artists' suppliers in various shades) into gum arabic, a watery adhesive which will fix the drops of metallic powder without dulling its brilliance, as oil-based media or varnishes do.

Spattering colours over a coloured base (which can be sponged, stippled or ragged for interest) allows you to arrive at a colour gradually with scope for correction at any stage. Fun to do if you do not have to worry about making a mess. Excellent on small items like lamps, frames and trays, and currently very fashionable. Over a large surface spattering is done faster by striking a colour-loaded brush (not too much) sharply against a stick.

RIGHT *One of the most talked about special finishes ever –
ridgy gesso, fluffed over with powder colour and accented
with wax. Unique, expensive and definitely not washable,
this finish demands sumptuous furnishings.*

FAR RIGHT *Bravura marbling in grey-white and rouge
roi colours, plus discreet trompe l'œil mouldings, gives
flat walls and surfaces a look of Second Empire splendour
in the champagne bar of the Sheraton Park Tower,
Knightsbridge.*

ABOVE *A close-up, showing how convincing well-painted
trompe l'œil details can be.*

UNDER-THE-BRUSH

This is a finish decorative painters might well use on their own walls. It is the freest and most painterly, its looping brushmarks creating a soft but highly textured surface. To subdue the busy pattern, painters tend to use a more opaque glaze than usual, that is, one where white undercoat predominates over commercial glaze. The proportions are somewhere between 2 to 1 and 1 to 1, depending on the colour used and the effect wanted. (For the sample board, see p. 53. Mark Hornak used a 2 to 1 mixture.)

Method

After the wet glaze is applied (two people are needed to paint a wall larger than 2.5 × 3.0 metres), it is distressed in a 'series of upward and downward flying curves, a sort of controlled chaos'. Mark Hornak uses a standard 75 mm paint brush. The stylishness of this particular finish consists in snapping off the ends of the curved brushmarks, at both the start and the finish of each stroke, so that they form little rainbows without blurred or trailing ends.

For those who prefer a more gentle effect, Mark suggests softening the surface with a badger blender or dust brush while the glaze is still wet. To make this finish completely matt, cover it with a final coat of extra pale, dead flat varnish.

SPONGING ON

Technically by far the easiest decorative finish to apply, sponged-on colour – which can be in the form of glaze, or thinned emulsion – makes for a mottled texture which can be crisp or blurred, depending on whether it is done over a white base or a coloured one. A clear pastel colour sponged onto a white base looks fresh and pretty, a cheering finish for a kitchen, bathroom or 'cottagey' bedroom. By using sophisticated colours, complex effects can be achieved. Sponging is a finish beginners can have fun with, as there is no problem with keeping the glaze wet.

Materials

An ocean sponge, in a size which fits comfortably into your hand, is the only special equipment needed. You should also have a flat plate to put the colour onto, and waste paper for testing prints.

Method

Sponging with a standard glaze mixture gives softer, transparent prints. First wring out the sponge in white spirit to soften it, then take up some glaze and experiment on paper until you get the right amount of colour. Pat the paper lightly – the prints should be clear, not splodgy.

Sponging with emulsion, which can be tinted with gouache or stainer, or used straight from the tin, gives stronger, opaque prints. You may want to thin the emulsion with a little water to make softer marks. Wring the sponge out in water before use – it should be just damp, not wet.

For one-colour sponging simply start at a corner and dab sponge prints over the wall surface. Sponging usually looks more attractive if the prints are applied randomly, leaving a varying amount of background colour showing through. Change the sponge round from time to time to vary the marks it makes.

When sponging in two or three colours it is best to leave more base coat showing through on the first colour. The finished effect should combine areas where the colours are mingled. Stand back now and then while applying second and third colours to judge the effect – add more colour if you are not satisfied with the balance.

Under-the-brush is the painters' paint finish, the song of the brush as it were. Great for rough walls, it may look like organized chaos initially, but it comes together the moment you hang a picture up, or when allied to characterful furnishings. The secret of under-the-brush is to keep the brushed arcs moving in different directions, but snap them on and off at the start and finish of strokes to avoid indecisive blurs.

SPONGING OFF

Method

This is really a rapid way of breaking up the surface of a standard emulsion paint to give a little texture. Use an ocean sponge again to give an irregularly blotched surface. The emulsion should be thinned a little with water, and brushed on a strip at a time. Then go over the wet paint with the sponge, dabbing at it to shift the paint around and mottle it. You may need to rinse the sponge out in clean water occasionally to clear off excess paint. Emulsion brushed on in this way dries to a slightly richer texture than usual, and makes a good background for stencils.

NEMONE BURGESS'S SQUARE SPONGE PRINTS

The overlapping gold-leaf squares which make up the background of Japanese screens gave Nemone Burgess the idea for this finish.

Method

A standard synthetic sponge is used to make the prints, overlapping at all the edges to suggest the effect of gold leaf. Foam sponges will give even prints, while holey, synthetic sponges will give more textured prints. Again, sponging with glaze will give softer prints than sponging with thinned emulsion. Nemone used a soft greyed-yellow with the gold leaf in mind, but it would look effective in almost any soft colour.

For the best results pour the glaze into a flat dish or a large foil freezer container, so the sponge can pick up colour evenly all over. Test on paper each time you renew the colour. Then simply press sponge prints across the wall, row after row, overlapping each print about 12 mm all round. Finish with clear matt varnish.

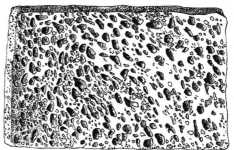

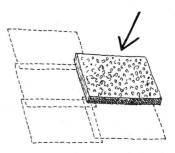

LEFT *Sponging is fun because you do not have to hurry to beat the drying time of wet glaze, and because you can step up the total colour effect gradually. Sponging can be sparse and naïve looking, or dense as in a pointilliste painting. For blurry effects, use a dampened sea sponge.*

ABOVE *Nemone Burgess discovered this offshoot of sponging which could look magnificent built up to suggest overlapping gold leaf, or just making quiet abstract shapes in a modern room. Press a synthetic sponge into wet glaze, overlapping prints to create a regular grid.*

GESSO AND DRY COLOUR

This is a truly virtuoso finish, not for beginners, though you might like to adapt some of the techniques and effects involved. Jim Smart invented it for its 'antiqued' appearance and extraordinary texture – at once ridgy and rough due to the brushed-out gesso, and deliciously soft and powdery due to the French chalk and dry colour. The toughest challenge it presents to an amateur is getting the gesso to the right consistency. If you are prepared to experiment until you master this, the rest is feasible.

I should add, however, that the uses for this finish are limited; by its very nature it can neither be sealed to protect it nor can it be washed to clean it.

Materials

You will need the following tools and materials: five 1-kilo bags of whiting and 1 kilo of rabbit skin glue granules (from artists' suppliers); 1 kilo of French chalk; dry powder colour in the shade you want – paler shades look best, but expect the powder colour to appear a couple of tones lighter on the wall than in the jar; a large hogs'-hair brush, preferably rounded like an old-fashioned painters' sash tool, for applying the gesso – the rounded clump of bristles will pick up more gesso; something soft and fluffy for applying the French chalk and dry colour, like a shaving brush, powder puff or cotton wool; several sheets of fine sandpaper; a very large double boiler arrangement or *bain-marie* for cooking up the gesso and keeping it warm; and a large bowl or bucket, preferably metal, not plastic.

Method

Tip 500 g of rabbit skin glue granules into the top of your double boiler, add 4.5 litres of water, and mix with a wooden spoon. Stand this in the bottom of the double boiler and heat the pan slowly, stirring the glue mixture till the granules are dissolved – do not rush this part. When the glue is hot and lump-free, turn the heat down a little, and tip 1 kilo of whiting into a large bowl or bucket. Stand this beside you and begin slowly crumbling handfuls of whiting into the glue. If you can sieve the whiting, so much the better. The object of this is to eliminate air bubbles and lumps, both of which could cause the gesso finish to crack later. Continue feeding whiting into the glue until it shows above the surface, then stir gently but firmly with a long-handled wooden spoon until you get a thick white mixture. The problem at this juncture is knowing if you have enough whiting in your glue to give a gesso mixture which is neither too thick, which means it will set too hard too fast, nor too thin, which means it will not stick fast enough to the wall surface.

The test is whether a layer forms on the surface after a period of gentle heating and stirring. It should form a skin, rather like jam, and develop a slightly brownish colour. A little gesso pressed between two fingertips should be tacky – not exactly sticky, just clinging. If all this fails to happen add more whiting, stir, and slowly heat again. Getting the gesso right can take up to an hour, but it should not be hurried, and the heat beneath the double boiler should be moderate only.

Having got the gesso to the right consistency, take the double boiler over to the wall surface. It is best to begin on the window wall, which is against the light. Dip the sash tool into the gesso and, at the top right-hand corner, quickly begin brushing down over the entire wall surface, keeping the brushstrokes going in the same direction. The gesso leaves a ridgy texture. Try to keep the coat even, moving quickly to avoid a pile-up, and roughing the surface with the brush

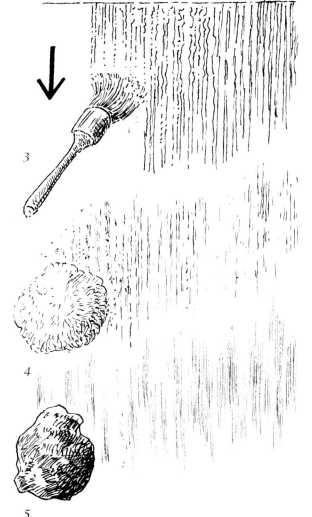

1,2

3

4

5

tip if it shows signs of hardening off. If the brushmarks get too heavy it means that the gesso is cooling too much and needs heating up gently again. Ideally, the *bain-marie* should be kept on a platewarmer to maintain an even temperature, but gesso must *never* boil.

Gesso brushed on like this will not take very long to dry hard. By the time all four walls have been covered, the first section will be ready for the next stage, which is less arduous and more intriguing.

Tip some French chalk into a saucer, and begin dusting it over the gesso surface, going with the grain or brushmarks, to coat it with this fine slippery substance. The chalk makes the dry colour cling more evenly – French chalk is dusted over wooden dance floors to make them slippier. When you have covered the entire wall surface, pick up some of the dry colour on a soft cloth or cotton wool, and stroke it over the gesso, again following the brushmarks. Start in a hidden corner so as to practise the next sequence of actions before embarking on the entire room. First chalk, then dry colour, then – and this is surprising perhaps – go over the whole surface with fine sandpaper, again with the grain. Magic-ally, this softens and refines the colour, as well as slightly smoothing the surface. The final touch, which is optional but gives a certain relieving sparkle to the gentle bloom of this finish, is to take a ball of beeswax and rub it lightly down the gesso ridges here and there.

FAKE FRESCO

There are many different ways of achieving the fresco effect, but they all seem to follow naturally after the gesso and dry colour look since their appeal has to do with a similarly dry, 'lean' finish on walls, and a gentle bloom of chalky colour. True fresco, used for painting walls from ancient

---

1 Rabbit skin glue being warmed until it dissolves in a bain-marie.

2 Whiting being sieved in, a handful at a time.

3 A round sash tool holds more gesso and makes ridgy brushmarks.

4 Fluffing on dry colour with cotton wool, a powder puff or a soft brush, again following the ridges.

5 Rubbing beeswax along the ridges.

Fine abrasive paper, rubbed down the brushmarks, will smooth and soften the colour.

RIGHT *Colourwashing in a soft, greyed, raw sienna makes an ideally unobtrusive but charming background to the cottage style – rush matting, stone flags and precise stencilling – of this tiny hall in the country.*

ABOVE *Ragging can look formal, an impressive foil to a handsome Victorian fireplace, dark picture frames and a strongly patterned Chinese pot. Here the colour is picked up in the marbled skirting board.*

BELOW *Years ahead of everyone else, this classic example of the faded fresco effect, decorated with 'grisaille' saplings, was designed by John Fowler for a small summerhouse.*

times, was the technically demanding process of applying colour to wet lime plaster, a patch at a time. Colour and plaster integrated as the patch dried to create an extremely durable surface with a peculiarly dry texture. The colour has a beautifully luminous quality.

Because true fresco is so exacting to do – mistakes are almost impossible to paint out – there is little demand for it today, even among the more sophisticated. Sometimes described as the 'crumbling palazzo' finish, the fake fresco look is still in the experimental stages, with all the more innovative decorative painters trying various approaches and combinations to suggest the real thing. It looks both old and ageless and gives great distinction to any room.

RUBBED-IN COLOUR :

This is my own version of the fresco effect, which has the charm of being immensely easy to do as well as giving characteristically diaphanous colour. As so often happens, I stumbled on the method accidentally (rubbing a mistaken glaze off a board), and though my own use of it has been successful, I feel it could still be improved upon.

Preparation

It is essential to have a slippery base coat – vinyl silk proved satisfactory in my case, but eggshell would probably be better. Any filling in of the wall surfaces needs to be thoroughly touched in, or sealed, with repeated coats of paint because the 'soak in' of colour is very pronounced, like great streaks and bruises, where the wall suddenly becomes porous. Slightly rough areas in the wall surface are less problematic because although the finish will reveal these, they do not look as ugly as they would on a shiny lacquer finish, but merely 'rough and old'.

Method

Use a mixture of solvent, commercial glaze and stainers plus a small amount of undercoat for the glaze, and tint it up to a very strong version of the desired colour. You need to have a very intensified version of your chosen colour as it will look much paler once it has been rubbed in. For the cloudy rose colour in my sitting room I mixed a tone close to mahogany red. The effect of a deep colour teased and rubbed to a pale blush is not the same as the pale blush colour thickly applied. The rubbing action not only makes the colour transparent, a mere film, but makes it settle a little irregularly. I used some dry powder colour in my mixture, which does help to give a 'lean' powdery look, but is a nuisance to use as the powder tends to settle at the bottom of the mixture and needs constant stirring to keep it dispersed. Experiment on a board coated with the same base paint till you get the colour right.

Application is simplicity itself. Using old rags, rub the colour quickly and firmly onto the wall, dispersing it as far as it will go while maintaining the right degree of colour. A circular polishing motion seems to work best, and it is very good exercise! The finish dries to a tough, washable surface with a very slight pearly sheen. To make it more matt, cover with extra pale, dead flat varnish.

ANCIENT RUBBED-AWAY COLOUR :

This is my own name for an effect which is highly unorthodox, but is worth mentioning because it makes walls, even new plasterwork, look as if they had been standing for thousands of years. It makes a splendid base for further painted decoration, like the mural in my own house. It would also enhance one of the sophisticated multi-layer stencils. An interesting feature of the finish is that while it looks rough and grainy, the wall surface will in fact emerge silky-smooth, an ideal surface for paint.

Method

The colour on the walls is what remains after 90 per cent of the paint has been sandpapered off, so you need to start with a very intense colour. I used a deep brownish-red made from a red matt emulsion tinted up with stainers. It looked like cocoa powder. It was put on very roughly with a roller, just covering the wall area with strips of dark red, spiking off in every direction. When dry, I went over it with sandpaper, coarse and then medium grade, rubbing really vigorously until all that was left was a fine glow of apricot, shading into red. It had a fascinating 'ancient' texture when examined closely where the darker red had been rubbed into all the little imperfections you find in any wall surface. The amount of colour in this finish depends entirely on how thoroughly you sandpaper. From time to time, stop to check the effect, standing back a few feet, because you might like more colour left, or a slightly more evened-out effect.

DEMI-SECCO:

This effect is achieved by applying a watery gouache colour over a 'thirsty' textured wall.

Materials

The base coat should be old-fashioned distemper, made from whiting or chalk, glue size and a preservative such as alum. This can be obtained in some circumstances from the Society for the Protection of Ancient Buildings (SPAB) who keep stocks of it for the restoration of old buildings. Oil-bound distemper is available commercially: it is less powdery than the classic distemper but much more durable.

Method

Mix up the wash using a little of the base coat and a lot of water, tinting with gouache colours. One colour brushed over a distempered wall will look charmingly natural, slightly dappled where the brushstrokes overlap. For a more antique, sophisticated look, try using two or three sympathetic washes of colour, dappling them irregularly over the walls and softening the overlaps a little with a dry brush. Not for the timid, this finish can look magnificent. Sealing with extra pale, dead flat varnish helps to prevent the powdery colour rubbing off, but the colour will look fresher without it.

DESIGNER IDEAS

" Scumbling technically involves using darker washes or glazes over paler colours, or paler washes or glazes over darker colours to create a chalky, fresco effect.

Designer Annabel Grey arrived at this technique almost fortuitously. One of her first commissions after leaving the Royal College textile department was a set of painted curtains. The curtains seemed to need more

painted effects to go with them, so Annabel designed a mural scheme for the whole room, taking her inspiration from the shapes and decorations of Etruscan and Roman pottery fragments. She knew exactly the effect she wanted: 'A matt, dull surface . . . old, not terribly intruding, quiet', and the method she used to achieve this was inspired by her work with textiles.

'Because I'm used to painting on fabrics with pigments which need a lot of dowsing with white if they aren't to look garish, I often end up with a chalky finish. I like that look, the colour just coming through the white. So that's how I did this room. When I wanted, say, a faint pink, I painted on a fierce, blinding red, and then put white on over that till I'd cooled it right down to a whisper. It was done by trial and error and instinct.'

In this way, her areas of tinted emulsion in violent fauve colours of orange, purple and red shine through a layer of thinned emulsion to emerge in the most subtle, ghostly fashion, quite distinct from each other but with all their heat tempered, as blocks of purest chalky pastel colour. More than anything, it

reminded me of ancient wall painting in churches, uncovered from layers of later lime-wash. What gives her muted decorations their special chic is the decisive contrast supplied by touches of Plaka gold and crisp black.

Annabel's work on this

elegant, distinctive room led directly to her being commissioned to design murals for the refurbishing of Marble Arch and Finsbury Park underground stations. **”**

COLOURWASHING

This finish derives from the weathered colour of rural buildings, and the special charm of earth colours which were once vivid, but have faded over the years. Anyone who has been struck by the beauty of Suffolk pink, or the bleached ochre and mellowed red oxides of Provence, will have noticed that exterior paints fade unevenly, and it is this finish that colourwashing attempts to reproduce – but indoors. Unlike 'under-the-brush', which is done with an oil-based glaze and looks distinctly textured, colourwashing uses water-based colour and aims for floating, uneven effects. It remains one of the prettiest treatments for cottage interiors. Any colour can be applied in this way: yellow through to apricot, pink and soft brick-reds, all give an incomparably warm, glowing look, while clear pale blue and green seem delicate and luminous.

Materials

The ideal base for colourwashing is a white distemper-type paint, as this has the right absorbent powdery texture. Oil-bound distemper is still available (see suppliers index), less powdery than the classic distemper but tougher and washable. Standard white matt emulsion can be substituted, too. Choose an off-white shade in preference to brilliant white, which has a blue cast to it that shows through a coloured wash. Whichever base paint you use, apply enough coats for the surface to look thick and evenly white – unevenness must come with the colour.

Method

The wash is made by tinting a little of the base coat paint with gouache colours, stainers or powder pigment. Powder pigment should not be used to colour oil-bound distemper because the powder does not dissolve properly when oil is present. It helps the powdery look, however, when mixed with standard emulsion, so you may like to experiment with it, but make sure you dissolve the powder first in water, grinding it with a pestle and mortar if necessary to refine the particles. The tinted paint is then diluted heavily with water to make a wash. When very watery, the colour is purer, but the wash trickles and is difficult to handle. Adding more paint makes it easier to manage but gives a more opaque, pasty colour because of the white content. As with most of these finishes, a little experimentation and rehearsal pays off.

Colourwashing is done in two stages to maximize the dappling of colour. Using a large bushy decorating brush (125 mm size), brush the coloured wash out in all directions, deliberately keeping it a little uneven so that some of the white base shows through in patches. Keep a second dry brush handy for catching the worst trickles of colour and softening them. When the first wash coat is quite dry, go over the walls again in the same loose, every-which-way fashion, covering the white surface this time and allowing colour to build up where several layers have been superimposed. It may look wild at this stage, but it will come together as it dries.

Because of the washy colour and uneven application, this is the finish that reflects back most light from a pale base. It has an unpretentious charm everyone likes, ideal for rustic settings.

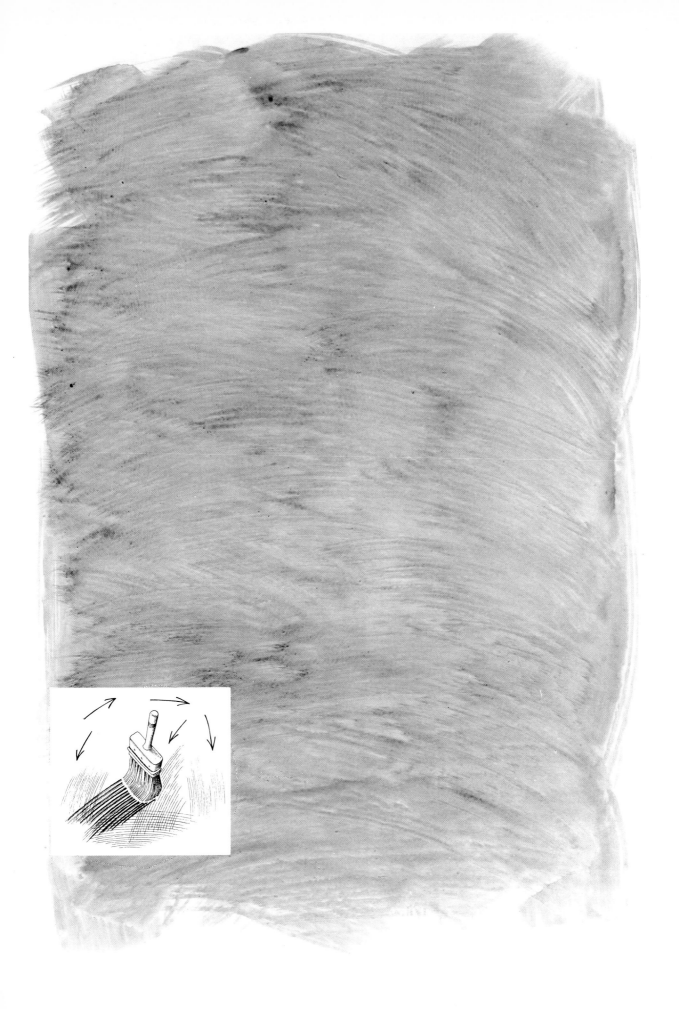

4

PAINTING THE WALLS II

Painting patterns on your walls by hand may seem a long way round when there are so many wallpapers to choose from, but anyone who covets a completely individual room will feel the results more than repay the time and effort involved. As with all painted decoration, the charm of painted pattern is that it can be tailor-made for your room. And of course you can have as much or as little of it as you want, from a discreet border to intricate, multi-layered stencilling covering the entire wall. If you live in an old house you might consider a stunning, but essentially simple harlequin pattern inspired by Florentine frescos. A cottage with uneven walls and low ceilings is the perfect setting for the primly charming stencil motifs that are derived from the American provincial tradition. A glum north-facing room can be made dazzling when decorated with the bold shapes and fauve colours associated with the Omega Workshop. Pattern need not be applied with a brush. It can be stamped, rolled or sprayed onto walls, using stencils or even an old cotton lace curtain to create a design.

Charleston Manor, home of Bloomsbury figures Vanessa Bell and Duncan Grant, is packed with examples of their exuberant decorative work. The colours sing, the textures breathe, the patterns look dashed on – it all has that casual vitality which amateurs never quite achieve. This is one of my favourite stencils ever, fresh and subtle, an updated Paisley.

Pattern appeals, I think, to a very basic human desire to impose order in a chaotic universe, and pattern-making must be one of the most ancient decorative impulses. It seems likely, from the universality of certain basic pattern rhythms – waves, spirals, zigzags – that pattern-making evolved from the repetition of mystic or magical symbols. We no longer recognize the original meaning of most of the patterns we use, but in view of the persistence of certain motifs perhaps their archetypal power registers at a subconscious level.

Pattern is decoration in its purest form, a repetition of aesthetically pleasing shapes which make surfaces rich and lively to look at without demanding the mental attention you would give to a picture. Most people find patterned walls easier to live with than picture-walls – and more satisfying than plain or textured walls. Pattern allows you to introduce more colour, but above all it involves movement, a dynamic rhythm of colour and shape which activates what would otherwise be static. Sophisticated patterns usually try to disguise the 'repeats', but I suspect that the repetition is one reason for the power of pattern. It is the visual equivalent of calming, repetitive sounds such as ticking clocks, heart beats and breaking waves.

Trying to invent new patterns is largely wasted effort. Even the greatest designers, like William Morris, were content to work with traditional elements, developing and refining them, introducing new colour combinations and reinterpreting old themes. Save your originality for colour and arrangement, and borrow motifs from any source that appeals to you. As stenciller Felicity Binyon firmly states, 'Inspiration is everywhere once you start to look.'

Old tiles, pottery, wrought iron grilles can all supply motifs for pattern-making. Spend an hour or so in a museum, sketching ideas that can be adapted for your own decorative use.

CRESSIDA BELL'S LEAF STAMP

This is one of those brilliantly simple ideas that someone else always thinks of first. Cressida Bell cut a leaf shape out of plastic foam and, dipping it into a vivid cerise matt vinyl emulsion, printed a whirling shower of leaves all over her bedroom walls.

If you copy this idea you should remember to vary the direction of your leaf prints – to keep them lively make them overlap or spiral round. Keep on printing after the colour begins to wear thin, because the contrast of colour and texture this gives is very attractive. Cressida could not resist adding squiggles to her leaves here and there with a gold felt-tipped pen. If you follow suit, be prepared to invest in several pens as the gold runs out quite rapidly.

THE DECORATIVE RUBBER STAMP

Derived from blockprinting on fabric, this idea comes via George Oakes of Colefax and Fowler, who stamped little green sprigs on the bathroom walls of his country cottage to create an innocently charming effect. I found my motifs in old Indian textiles, and they are reproduced here, drawn to scale, for anyone to copy them. They can be turned into rubber stamps by any reasonably enterprising rubber stamp manufacturer for a modest price. Varying your pattern with stamps in two different sizes, as George Oakes did, will give your pattern twice as much liveliness.

Materials

There are a number of different types of paint that you can use: acrylics are handy, but they tend to dry rapidly; Plaka water-based paints are quite easy to use, but take care not to smudge them; printing inks pick up and print nicely, but, again, take care not to smudge them while they are drying; signwriters' colours (see suppliers index) behave well and dry fast. Keep a small pane of glass handy for spreading colour onto; a flat plate will do just as well.

Method

You can pencil lightly where you propose to stamp, but I do not think it is necessary for most patterns. A simple grid looks best, alternating large and small motifs, and staggering each row so that the motifs are spaced halfway between those in the rows above and below. A painted ribbon of the same colour neatens up wall edges prettily.

Anyone who has used a commercial rubber stamp will know just how to set about printing patterns. The only things to watch out for are taking up too much paint on the stamp, which creates a blurred impression, and allowing the colour on the plate or glass to dry up. If it does, add a few drops of water or white spirit, depending on the base of your paint.

All these designs, inspired by old textile blocks, would reproduce well as decorative rubber stamps.

STRIPES

Broad stripes in clear, gentle colours, like the ones shown in Cressida Bell's flat, are tranquilly decorative, easy to do and suit most rooms. Cressida used standard matt emulsion, tinting and mixing until she got the right colour values for her stripes.

Method

A plumb line and masking tape make easy work of getting the stripes tidy and vertical. Remove excess adhesive from the tape by attaching it to another surface, then peeling it off before fixing it to the next wall. This avoids fall-out when you finally remove it. In rooms with coved or pitched ceilings, such as attics, the stripes can be taken up over the ceiling for a tented effect.

ABOVE *A repro Georgian fire surround, picked out in a pale orange colour, was inspired by an Omega Workshop piece (Vanessa Bell was Cressida's grandmother).*

LEFT *A simple leaf shape and oddments of coloured emulsions produced this riot of colour in her bedroom.*

RIGHT *Cressida Bell's painted stripes are wider and the colours are warmer than Nemone Burgess's (see p. 24), but they work to make a gentle yet striking background to her own stunning prints.*

CRESSIDA BELL

FREEHAND PATTERN BLOCKS

When painting my kitchen walls, I decided not to translate the pattern into stencils, which would have given a regular effect, preferring the variety of a freehand approach. The blocks of pattern, repeated over the wall, make a very positive impact (see p. 20).

Method

Marking out beforehand is less critical with rectangular blocks. I pencilled in key vertical and horizontal lines and cut a template the size of the blocks. A steel rule and plumb line always make marking out easier. I added the ground colour, a dirty ochre yellow (I mixed in some turmeric for a laugh – it worked), to standard white emulsion, thinned with water to a milky consistency, and brushed it on roughly to give an aged look. The red and black pattern blocks are painted in acrylic colours, also thinned slightly with water, and applied with stubby artists' brushes. The walls were finished with two coats of yacht varnish, the toughest varnish available, which sealed the decoration against the steam and smoke of kitchen life.

HARLEQUIN DIAMONDS

Bold designs like this were often used for the walls of late medieval Italian palaces and castles, especially in Florence, where they would have been painted in fresco. This dries to a fine matt surface, leaving the colour clear but soft – the use of standard opaque paints would make such patterns appear too harsh. Leonard Lassalle used his favourite technique of pure artists' pigment over oil-bound distemper which gives much the same effect (see p. 112). Anyone trying a design like this should follow suit. For the detailed painting, such as the frieze over the bookcases and the witty trompe l'œil cat, Leonard used his other favourite medium – egg tempera (see p. 111).

Method

Geometric patterns need rather careful measuring and marking out in pencil or chalk before painting. Diagonals are tricky because a line which is only a couple of degrees out at the base of a wall will have wandered noticeably further afield by the time it reaches the top. And when you are using three transparent washes of colour, mistakes can only be rectified by painting out with the white base and starting all over again. Note Leonard's use of white between the coloured diamonds; it helps to soften the contrast between two strong complementary hues. You might perhaps try this design in the delicate pastel colours of the traditional harlequin costume – you would not need the white buffer zone for this, but care should be taken to keep the colour values similar. It would be a good idea to research some actual examples – ballet designs, paintings of masquerades or carnivals, for instance.

STENCILLED PATTERN

Stencilling has become deservedly popular since designers such as Cile Lord in America and Lyn Le Grice in Britain pioneered the revival of this ancient decorative craft almost a decade ago. These two, in their turn, owe a great deal to the inspiration of a remarkable lady. Janet Waring, who tracked down surviving examples of early nineteenth-century stencilling in New England and recorded them in a classic book – *Early American Stencils* – published in the thirties.

Stencils are creativity without tears, a simple and straightforward means of adding pattern to walls, floors, furniture and fabric. They have been used since the time of the pharaohs, at least. A stencil consists, essentially, of a decorative cut-out in some paint-proof material (for example, leather, thin metal, oiled card or paper and acetate) through which paint can be brushed, sponged, sprayed or dabbed onto the surface beneath. Their first use was to speed up the process of repetitive decoration – an early form of mass-production. Ironically, their popularity to-day stems largely from a reaction *against* mass-production. People like their stencilling to look a little irregular, perhaps unevenly coloured, for that very reason. Wallpaper firms are producing papers with a stencilled look, but hand-painted stencilling still has more class.

It is possible, given skill and patience, to reproduce any design with stencils, even filigree patterns of such complexity as Mary MacCarthy's bravura stencilled 'marquetry'. The bold foliage and colouring of Jacobean crewel-work can be recreated on the walls of a cottage bedroom, though this may involve using more than thirty separate stencils. Elaborate patterns take longer to build up, simply because they require more stencils – one per colour. The process itself

A chinoiserie stencil designed by Stewart Walton. Try it in gold on dark painted furniture, or in colour on walls.

Leonard Lassalle uses egg tempera, one of the oldest and toughest of painting media, for these strong, colourful murals inspired by Tudor and Jacobean crewel work. They make vivid settings for the virile oak furniture in which he specialises. Against a dark ground, Leonard first paints in the design with white distemper, later applying egg tempera colours which he mixes himself.

BELOW A close-up detail shows the loose, confident nature of this technique; nothing is fussy or worked over.

remains the same and is largely mechanical, although artistic judgement obviously comes into the choice of colours and arrangement of motifs. In keeping with the current tendency towards polychrome decoration, the trend in stencilling is towards greater intricacy, with whole teams of decorators working for weeks to give walls ravishing subtleties of pattern and colour. There is nothing to prevent you from aiming at a similar effect, building up the pattern over the course of months by adding to it in spare moments.

Beginners, impatient for results, can now choose from quite a good range of pre-cut, or ready-to-cut, stencils. There is even a small but thriving shop devoted entirely to the craft (see suppliers index). These stencils are mostly in simple folk style, with florals predominating. Lyn Le Grice, however, has recently added some sophisticated chinoiserie-inspired designs to her range of stencils.

All the same, it is a pity not to try designing and cutting your own stencils because mastering the simple principles of this technique puts a useful decorative tool at your fingertips and makes so many more effects possible.

SIMPLE STENCILS:

Simple does not necessarily mean 'naive' in the style of the early American folk designs. Both Cressida Bell's fleur-de-lys stencil on a stone-coloured ground and Graham Carr's striking blue chinoiserie stencils (see p. 108) are simple in the sense that they use only one colour and one motif, spaced out on a grid. These designs were inspired by old textiles, one of the richest sources of suitable motifs.

Others might include embroideries, heraldic designs or lace. Photocopying makes light work of enlarging designs to the right size for use on a wall.

The classic 'gul' or pine motif as seen on the cover, used on Kashmiri and later Paisley shawls, is here translated into a stencil for you to copy. Enlarge or reduce the size as required.

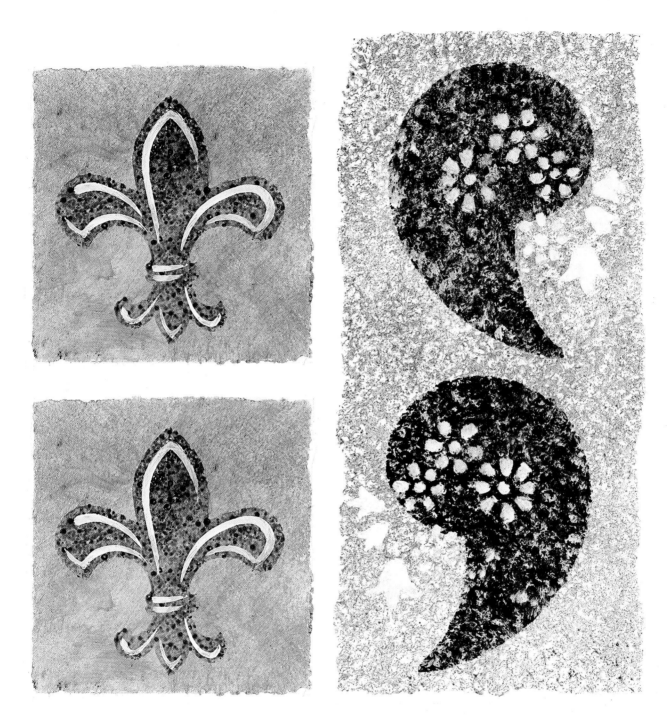

Cressida Bell's simple but effective fleur-de-lys stencil, for which you need two stencils: one for the shape, the other for detail.

This stencil, based on the Charleston motif, contrasts springlike sprays of white flowers with roughly sponged 'comma' shapes beneath.

Graham Carr's stencilling is very distinctive. He likes to use large, loose motifs and sludgy colours, neatened off with painted bands. Tone and texture constantly vary, creating added vivacity. Graham has since washed over these walls in a drab yellow to make the room look warmer and more integrated.

When I described a stencil as a decorative cut-out, I was giving the simplest description possible; few shapes are both simple and decorative enough to be reduced to a single cut-out. A leaf or a cockle shell, perhaps, has impact as a silhouette, but most of the objects you might want to turn into stencils – flowers, birds, butterflies, trees and toys – need to be broken down further into visually and logically convincing elements. A rose silhouette looks much like a cabbage. To make it unmistakably a rose, the way the petals unfurl around the stamens needs to be indicated as simply and graphically as possible. You will note that the petals have to be stylized for the stencil to hold together. It becomes a series of petal-shaped holes connected to the body of the stencil by a web of little 'bridges'. These bridges, or 'ties' as they are called, are what you usually have to introduce when transferring patterns into stencils. As you can see from the rose stencil, the ties show in the finished effect as outlines. The image is one-dimensional, a characteristic stencil effect. A simple way to give the rose, or any other three-dimensional object, more roundness and greater naturalism is to shade it with a little darker colour. This does not have to be added carefully as if you were painting a portrait of a real rose – just a few touches rapidly applied will suffice. It is possible, by building up the rose with several separate stencils, to produce an entirely naturalistic flower – but the process would be so lengthy it would be easier to paint the rose freehand.

Materials

To make the stencil you will need stencil card or acetate (though thick varnished paper will do), tracing paper, carbon paper and a Stanley knife or craft knife, with several spare blades. Japanese stencils use ties of a single thread and are supremely naturalistic, but fragile.

The skill of designing a stencil lies in creating expressive but functional 'ties', which turn what would otherwise be a silhouette into a recognisable motif.

Method

To enlarge or reduce a pattern or motif, trace it and then have the tracing put through a photocopying machine. Using carbon paper, trace this onto your stencil board, or, if using acetate, put the clear sheet on top and use a Rotring pen or chinagraph pencil to trace round the shape. Cut round the stencil shapes as clearly as possible. It is best to do this on a waste sheet of plywood that you can score into, or a pane of glass. Leave a couple of inches of board or acetate round the cut-outs for strength because stencils have to be handled frequently. If the stencil is for a border, leave enough board to align the pattern against the cornice or ceiling. It is a sensible precaution to start by stencilling your pattern onto another piece of board which you can keep as a spare, in case the first one gets torn, or clogged with paint.

The best paints to use are fast drying to obviate smudging. Artists' acrylic colours dry almost instantly and the colour range is enormous. Many professionals, like Felicity Binyon and Liz Macfarlane, use signwriters' paints because they claim the colours are livelier and less 'plastic'. They also dry very quickly. What you use to apply the paint depends on the effect you want. You can brush the colour on using a brush with short, thick bristles; then use a stencil brush, with a stippling action, for shading. Alternatively, you can use only stencil brushes. A sponge is a very quick way of appplying the colour, although aerosol paint in cans, as used by Lyn Le Grice, is obviously the speediest and least tiring method. This, however, has the disadvantage of having to mask the surrounding surface.

Stencilled colour can be applied to most surfaces. Matt surfaces look best, although stencilling matt colour onto a shiny base gives a damask effect which can be very attractive. Opinions are divided as to whether the base colour beneath should be distressed or plain. There is a conven-

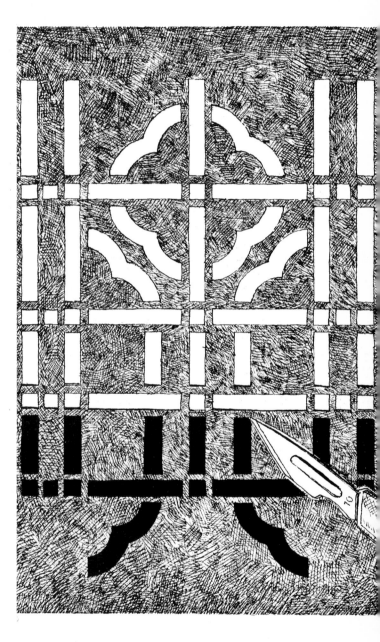

Use a sharp scalpel blade to cut your stencil; cutting at an angle gives a bevelled edge, the mark of an ace stencil cutter.

BELOW *Standing on this bedroom mantelpiece, beside a Quentin Bell sculpture, is a terracotta vase, decorated to match the room using acrylic colour and a glaze of polyurethane, white spirit and stainer.*

LEFT *Painted with a mixture of a signwriters' paint and eggshell, and then glazed, Botticcelli's* Birth of Venus *covers one bedroom wall. The calico curtains and bedspread are painted with Procian's watercolour, their dyes and design achieved with a wax technique. Even the lampshade has been painted.*

tion that folk stencils of the early American variety, are applied onto plain, flat colour to keep the effect simple. I personally prefer the look of a lightly distressed background – sponged, stippled or colourwashed – for almost all stencilling.

Applying colour

Squeeze a little colour into a saucer. You need much less than you would believe possible. Work the brush bristles into the colour, and try it out on a sheet of waste paper. The best results are achieved with very little colour, worked to a fine film; thick colour looks clogged and tends to creep under the stencil. Complicated, fragile stencils may need to be fixed in place with masking tape or tacks to hold them steady, but simpler examples can usually be positioned with

one hand while you stencil with the other. Again, practise on waste paper first. If your simple stencil requires two colours, one for a flower, say, and one for the leaves, you will find it easier to do these separately. Shading likewise can be added the second time around. By then you will be able to judge how your pattern is developing.

Registration of stencils

With any continuous pattern, like a border, you need to work out a way of ensuring that you begin a new section exactly where the last one ended. Clear acetate eliminates this problem, but on a stencil board you can either cut nicks in the stencil edge or arrange the stencil so that the pattern begins and ends on the same motif.

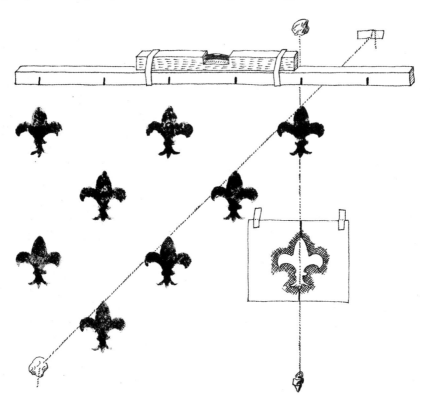

Elaborate stencils

If you want to reproduce a complex pattern like a rug design, which uses several colours, you will need several stencils. Stewart Walton liked the pattern of his sitting room rug so much he decided to use it as the basis of a stencil pattern for the walls. As you can see by comparing the original rug with the finished stencil (see p. 108), he has simplified the pattern and altered the colours. But the stencil retains the spirit and boldness of the handwoven rug. He cut five separate stencils, using one main motif from the rug. It would have been too much of an undertaking to try and reproduce them all. Having chosen his motif, he speeded up the process by plotting out his pattern on the largest sheet of stencil board available, cutting it out several times over to correspond with the way in which the pattern was to develop on the wall. This enabled him accurately to locate the motifs, and complete half a dozen at one go instead of having to measure and check each time as he would have done with a single-motif stencil. He cut two separate, smaller stencils for details, another large one for the bold outlines, and one more for the grid design which links the motifs together.

Stewart used acrylic colours for his stencil, diluted in a little water, to which he added some PVA adhesive (see suppliers' index) as a binder. The PVA allows the acrylic colour to be thinned down to a transparent solution without becoming too watery. To compensate for a simplified colour scheme, he rang the changes on his three basic colours, painting the motif red and details blue the first time, and then reversing the colour scheme the second time. For further variety he changed the texture of the stencilling as the mood took him, either stippling it with a brush, sponging it or ragging it. Tricks like these enrich the final effect for only a little more effort. Overlaying transparent colours on the principal motif also

Working out a grid for stencils on walls needs accurate measuring, but you can use primitive equipment – cotton and Blu-tack, string and a plumb line, or a wooden batten sectioned off at measured intervals. However carefully you measure, do not despise your 'eye' – not all walls are vertical, straight or flat.

This simplified motif, abstracted from an elaborately patterned rug, led via changes of colour to the richly patterned walls in Stewart Walton's own sitting room (see also p. 108).

FAR RIGHT *Not strictly painted, but too decorative to leave out – a tiny yellow painted bar-cupboard, the walls tricked out with black and white prints pasted onto the surface and framed with borders and bows sold through the National Trust.*

TOP *Very simple but effective, Cressida Bell's front hall with its fleur-de-lys motif in mauve-grey on creamy pink.*

CENTRE *Carolyn Warrender enjoys the demureness of early American stencil motifs like these, which she sells in her London stencil shop and combines in various colourways on the walls.*

BELOW RIGHT *More Graham Carr stencilling, bold and closely patterned in good 'dirty' colours. Here the base colour is warmer than before, the design consciously chinoiserie.*

BELOW *Details of Stewart Walton's rug (right) and the stencilled wall (left), showing how a change of colour can stretch the decorative power of a simple, repeated motif.*

introduced a random effect where red over blue created mauve. If you did not want this surprise element, you could use an opaque mix of colour for the superimposed detail.

Stencilling a complex pattern over an entire room is not something to try and cram into a weekend. The realistic approach is to expect it to grow gradually, adding more as and when you feel like it. If you can enlist the services of a helper so much the better; stencilling is pleasant when it is convivial, and when you are enjoying your work progress always seems faster. Do not worry if the colours are not exactly the same each time. Busy stencilled schemes usually look more attractive with some colour variation. You do not want to go to all that trouble and end up with a wall finish that looks like wallpaper. Interior designer John Stefanides had the walls of his sitting room stencilled in imitation of old embroideries, which meant capitalizing on subtle colour variations. First, the background was distressed with patchily applied glazes; transparent colour was used for the stencils, and varied just a little to suggest fading. In some places the pattern was rubbed off slightly with wire wool to look worn. This may sound like a lot of work, but the effect of walls covered with beautiful old fabric is entirely convincing and much admired.

Large patterns like these cover the ground faster. The really laborious stencil schemes are those which reproduce small-scale motifs, especially regular ones. A trellis with climbing plants would be a standard example. These depend on exact measuring up and marking out, and careful execution.

However, one attractive effect can be obtained quite easily by stencilling with an oil-based paint on a matt emulsion surface, and then brushing a tinted wash over the whole surface. Oil repels water, so the colour wash builds up round the outer edge of the stencilled pattern, while hardly altering the stencil at all. Pale colours applied on a white base create an effect like old damask or brocade. Use a slightly thinned gloss paint to stencil with as this will emphasize the textural contrasts. Silky, rather than shiny patterns will emerge against a matt background.

Background for stencilling

Stencilling tends to be done on a pale ground, but it can look dramatic over a darker base. The simple way to do this is to stencil in a positive colour several tones darker than the ground colour – midnight-blue over pale red, for instance, or brown on bamboo. This gives something of a Toile de Jouy effect, distinguished without being too colourful. But if you want colour, like the vividness of an old chintz against a dark background, you must first stencil all the designs in white, and then stencil colour on top. Leonard Lassalle's crewel-style mural painting (see p. 96–7) shows how effective this can be, although this was painted freehand.

Mary MacCarthy has stencilled her bathroom with floral and leaf motifs in soft greyed pastels, bordering directly onto the thistle-pink plaster. This looks very attractive, and is a good idea to copy, but the plaster will need sealing with diluted Unibond to prevent grease marks showing – even fingerprints can be greasy.

Protecting stencils

Extra pale, dead flat varnish will protect any stencilled scheme without adding shine or altering the colours, and this is the most popular finish among professionals. It gives sufficient protection for walls which do not need frequent washing-down. The shinier grades of varnish, eggshell or gloss give more protection for bathrooms, kitchens and hallways. Toughest of all is yacht varnish, which definitely darkens and yellows the colours beneath. This can be a bonus, ageing everything instantly with an amber film. If you like this effect, but not the shine it builds up, yacht varnish can be rubbed over with fine wire wool to cut the gleam, but give the walls at least two coats of varnish first, otherwise you are liable to cut through the varnish itself to the paint beneath. Lubricate the wire wool by rubbing it on a bar of soap, and wipe the walls over afterwards with a damp rag.

Shading Stencils

Shading can bring stencilled patterns to life. Certain motifs can be greatly enhanced by a suggestion of 3-D modelling: fruit, flowers, architectural subjects, urns and columns, for instance. Shaded fruit and flowers can look effective without being done in naturalistic colours, and shading does not have to be stippled on with the realism of a Dutch still life. Lyn Le Grice shades a lot of her work with spray paint, which she focusses on the area in question from a distance, so that the spray is fine enough to control. This gives a professional smoothness almost like airbrushing. Liz MacFarlane and Felicity Binyon shade with stencil brushes, stippling colour where they want to suggest roundness. Architectural subjects are usually done in *grisaille* or monochrome, or sometimes stony colours such as grey, beige or black.

EGG TEMPERA

It is a striking feature of the current decorative scene that so many painters are being inspired to imitate or revive old techniques. In many cases they begin experimenting out of curiosity, but stay with these methods because they can achieve effects obtainable in no other way. Leonard Lassalle uses egg tempera, one of the oldest painting media of all, for his mural painting because he likes its 'gentle, transparent colours, like watercolour', plus the paradoxical fact that 'it gets harder and harder with time – it lasts for ever.'

It is possible to buy tempera-type paints in some artists' ranges, but being a down-to-earth Frenchman he prefers to make his own. The materials are of the simplest kind.

Materials

His recipe begins, jokingly, 'grab a chicken' – you *do* need a fresh egg. Break the egg in half, so you can use the rounder half as a measure. Separate the yolk from the white, and roll the yolk on newspaper gently to mop up any remaining albumen. Then, with care, break the yolk membrane over a jam jar so that the yolk itself drops in, but not the membrane. Add 1 half-egg measure of raw linseed oil and $2\frac{1}{2}$ measures of distilled water. Screw on the lid and shake vigorously until the contents form a creamy emulsion. At this point add Leonard's secret ingredient – a few drops of surgical spirit. This not only stops the egg going off, but helps it to dry faster. 'It took me six months to discover this', he said. Into the tempera base, Leonard mixes artists' quality powder pigments, which can be found in a good artists' suppliers and are the purest form of colour available. Egg tempera painting needs no varnishing. Small ceramic palettes, with round hollows in them, are good for mixing up colours.

For murals like his colourful crewel-type designs on a dark ground (see p. 96–7), a special underpainting is needed because the tempera colour, being semi-transparent, is lost on a dark base. Having sketched out the design, Leonard paints it onto the dark base in white oil-bound distemper. You could substitute white undercoat. Over a white base the tempera colours glow beautifully, and the whole effect on a dark ground has the dazzle of vibrant embroidery.

DESIGNER IDEAS

" Leonard Lassalle is an antique dealer and artist who specializes in Tudor and Jacobean furniture. He began by decorating his own shop in Tunbridge Wells because he wanted to get the right sort of setting for the furniture. Soon clients began asking him if he would re-create for them his simple but vibrantly coloured effects; walls boldly colourwashed with emphatic texture, vivid murals based on crewel work, Florentine-inspired interiors painted in strong lozenges of colour. He now spends as much time designing and painting rooms in his individual style as he does running his business. The Lassalle approach is refreshing, owing as much to his knowledge of French and Italian traditions (he buys a lot of his paint colours abroad) as to his painterly sense of what suits the heavily beamed farmhouses and cottages of Kent.

'I use an oil-bound distemper which comes in big tubs [see suppliers index] for the base coat on my walls. It is not an easy paint to use as it is heavy to brush out, but the way the brushstrokes cross makes for a texture which gives patination in the final result. I use pure pigment for colouring, dry artists' colours (see suppliers index), because I cannot find any other colour that has that vibration. Modern colours are dyes, whereas mine, if you look at them under the microscope, are tiny particles of real earth. I use ferrous colours like the oxides. In France and Italy you can buy very good colours which are used for staining cement. I mix my colours in water in a jam jar, adding a very little distemper and shaking long and hard to dissolve it. Then I tip some colour into a bowl and apply it to the wall using a wide, floppy-bristled brush which I keep wet. The powder pigment I use is very strong and the distemper soaks it up, so I have to check to see that it is diluted enough to give the degree of colour that I want. I also have an old rag in the other hand, which I use to spread the colour that I have brushed on, and soften it as necessary. Putting on the colour takes no time at all, maybe one and a half hours for a room 35 metres square.'

This method is designed to put character and colour

back into early houses, built before eighteenth-century urbanity and 'good taste' persuaded people to plaster over their stud beams and timbered ceilings. It is a 'peasant' look, virile and unpretentious, which is more appropriate to tough vernacular building than the suave, polished finishes like ragging and dragging. These suit rooms built in the neo-classical tradition and later. It has become standard practice to paint the plastered surfaces in beamed rooms white, or at the most, shell-pink. But rich, positive colours, brushed on casually in the Lassalle manner, not only make these rooms look more coherent, but are, I suspect, more historically accurate. Limewashing in white may have been the usual finish for old plaster in poorer dwellings, but colour and pattern were invariably introduced as soon as house-owners could afford display. Surviving fragments of early plastered infills in beamed dwellings are often painted with bold herringbone stripes or floral patterns in strong colours. **"**

ROLLED-ON PATTERN

The easiest way to achieve this finish is with specially made rollers which are sold with detachable plastic roller heads. These are embossed with a variety of patterns, mostly floral. In many rural parts of Europe, colourwashed walls are still patterned in this way in imitation of wallpaper, which is either too expensive or too difficult to get hold of.

Colourways

Walls should be rolled in a darker tone of the base colour for the most telling effect: for example, gitane blue on a base washed over with a thinned-down pale blue colour. This looks attractive without being pretentious – something you should avoid if you want the full provincial nostalgia to show through. There is one exception to this rule: rolling white over a pastel colour gives a wonderfully frothy lace effect.

Method

Assemble the roller as shown on the pack, filling the container with standard matt emulsion. Begin rolling from the top of the wall downwards (if you roll across the wall, the paint will pour out of the container). Then repeat, immediately next to the first patterned stripe, and continue until the whole wall is covered. Some patterns require matching up at the seams – check by trying them out on a board – but most do not. Try to keep your rolling steady and straight; the odd wobble or swerve hardly shows in the final result, however. If you are concerned about this, use a plumb line as a guide.

Ordinary foam rollers, preferably the stiffer variety, can be cut with a scalpel to make bands of bold, African-looking pattern. Dip the roller in the paint (again standard emulsion is best, tinted with stainers if you wish) and then roll it on paper to remove the excess before applying it to the wall. The advantage of these rollers is that they can be rolled sideways as well, but they do run out of paint very quickly.

Deco-roller heads come in more than twenty different patterns. The deco-roller feeds paint via the rollers which print patterns simultaneously. It can be done upwards or downwards, but not sideways – or the paint falls out.

SPRAYED PATTERN

Dazzlingly easy and dashingly impressive, this finish can transform the walls of a small bathroom, for instance. Spray colour through a coarse cotton lace curtain, bought for next to nothing in street markets. The paint passes through the open mesh but not the finer woven pattern. It is hard to believe it will work, but it does, creating an instant brocade effect. Play this up by choosing suitable colours – sludge green on palest pink, brown on grey.

Materials

You can use the sort of spray paint sold for touching-up car bodywork (of which you will need several cans), and this comes in a huge range of colours, including metallics. The fumes are powerful, so work with the windows open and wear a mask. Alternatively, borrow or hire a spraying attachment which can be used with standard DIY paints.

Method

The lace can be tin-tacked or stapled in place each time – stretch it taut and close to the surface of the wall. Spray evenly, covering the whole piece of lace. It is as well to mask off each side with newspaper and Blu-Tack to catch paint. Eventually, the finer mesh in the lace will clog up with paint. One solution would be to get more than one length of the same pattern. If you are using a standard DIY paint, you can rinse out the lace in white spirit.

Spraying through lace can create wonderfully varied and opulent patterns on the surfaces beneath, almost without trying. Spray paints should be applied at the prescribed distance, with the surround masked off.

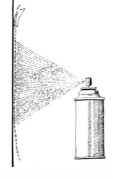

5

PAINTING THE FRAME

If pattern answers our need for ordered surfaces, a concern for proportion answers an equally powerful desire for ordered spaces. Ceilings that are too high, the unbalanced placing of windows, the bland results of stripping-out architectural elements – all these are vaguely disquieting, not so much positively wrong as not quite right. We feel comfortable in rooms with a clearly defined framework, with points of reference that allow us to orientate ourselves in a particular space. Just what module makes for the most convincing proportions, and why, is a mystery architects have pondered over since classical times. Probably it all comes back to that yardstick we all share, the human body. That wonderfully proportioned creation, the classical column, has three divisions – base, shaft and entablature – which can be seen as corresponding to legs, trunk and head. Traditional rooms have their walls sectioned off into three parts, like a column unrolled, and strike us as humanly-scaled however vast and palatial they may be. Rooms which are grounded with skirting and dado spell security, and a sense of place.

In an otherwise giddy space, a firmly painted cornice
finishing off a cloudy-grey marbled wall makes room
proportions manageable and supplies a visual 'framework'.
Beautifully handled paint finishes make something elegant
from an impossibly tricky hallway in a London flat – a
lesson in how paint can make a silk purse from
a sow's ear.

Not many people are lucky enough to live in classically-proportioned rooms, but there is a lot that can be done to rectify awkward spaces, restore harmony and introduce 'firmness'. (The classical objectives of architecture were summed up by the Elizabethan scholar, diplomat and architectural thinker, Sir Henry Wootton, as 'commodity, firmness and delight'.) Our eyes can be deceived: a painted line can stand in very satisfactorily for a dado, a stencilled frieze might substitute for a cornice, while high ceilings can be visually lowered and intrusive room fittings 'faded out' using nothing but artful paint.

Painted 'architecture' is one way of improving or correcting unsatisfactory proportions. Another, which has an equally respectable classical pedigree, is the use of colour to emphasize the three-dimensional aspect of a room, a box with a base and a lid as well as sides. The great designers, whether we are talking of Adam, Palladio or Mies van der Rohe, conceived of rooms in the round. The Adam library at Kenwood has a painted stucco ceiling and a carpet which picks up the ceiling design. The elaboration of these surfaces ensures that they are seen as continuous with the richly treated walls; substitute a plain white, flat ceiling and plain wall-to-wall carpet and the magnificent apartment falls apart. The same principle holds good in our own rooms. Enriching one set of surfaces – the walls, for instance – calls for a corresponding intensification of the others. One aspect of the decorative painting bonanza which has taken even the professionals by surprise is the number of commissions now received for painted ceilings, floors, and the elaboration of joinery and plasterwork which define the room space. The white woodwork and ceilings and plain fitted carpets that we are used to seeing are too neutral to be an effective surrounding for polychromatic patterned walls. In one way or another it is possible to apply most of the painting techniques that we have already discussed to the framework of the room. Wooden surfaces can be treated with stains and varnishes to create an array of wonderful effects – even the ceiling can become an excitingly patterned and textured element.

FLOORS
COMBING:

Combed colour gives floors a jolly, liquorice all-sorts look. It is an easy finish to do and is popular with DIY enthusiasts. Rustic spaces, such as converted barns or lofts and big family kitchens, are ideal locations.

Materials

For the combs choose from a wide range of home-made equipment: a length of plastic with zigzag teeth cut into it; a rubber squeegee notched in the same way (this is particularly handy because of the handle); an Afro comb.

Method

It is easiest to comb plywood squares separately, laying them down afterwards, because then there is no problem keeping within the square. If you do comb your squares straight onto a floor, you will probably need to tidy them around the edges. Paint your floor in two stages – every alternate square the first time, the rest after the first squares have dried. Almost any paint can be used for a combed surface (including emulsion), but the base needs to be a little slippery to comb smoothly. Give it a coat of gloss or eggshell paint, or varnish it if the paint is matt. Pale colour mixtures, such as green on yellow or buff on white, are popular and attractive.

Paint on a coat of your top colour, evenly and thickly. Then with your instrument comb it across in straight lines, wavy lines, or art deco intersecting arcs. Combing allows the base colour to show through and over a floor area creates a subtle but definite build-up of texture. When dry, varnish as usual.

STAINS AND VARNISHES:

After years of wall-to-wall carpeting the pendulum is swinging the other way. The lively texture of bare wood floors, perhaps decorated with painted patterns, is popular again. Nothing looks more warmly dignified than a floor of solid, smoothly polished boards.

Preparation

Unfortunately, when you take up carpets you are more likely to find a patchwork of planking: partially stained, discoloured, peppered with nail holes and tack heads. Even so, it is astonishing how gratefully timber responds to a beauty treatment. The first step is to go over the entire surface with a sanding machine. The logical time to do this is after building operations and before the last stages of decorating because sanding covers every surface with fine dust. It is better to sand floors over lightly – just enough to remove the topmost layer – rather than to grind away until the wood looks quite new again, as was done in the sixties.

Method

Having cleared the decks, as it were, the next thing to decide is whether the floorboards need remedial treatment, and if so, what kind. Floors can be stained in a whole range of colours, they can be lightened by rubbing in paint, or even painted over completely and decorated with stencils, or combed patterns. If the timber is quite presentable but you feel the need for a little colour, a coloured varnish stain (see suppliers index) is the easiest solution. Being transparent the varnish stain allows the wood grain to show through, which is attractive. For deeper colour, apply more coats; alternatively, combine two different colours for an interesting effect.

A fashionable transparent grey finish could be a good way round the problem of scruffy old floorboards. Apply a diluted black stain and go over this with a matt varnish to which a little white paint has been added. It is important to start with the right black: as blacks are diluted, strong undertones of either red or blue tend to show up. A combination of both tones is best, giving a soft but warm grey. Stains can be either spirit- or water-based (see suppliers index). Test on spare wood until you get the right shade, remembering that the final white-tinted varnish will lighten the effect a little, softening and cooling the stain. Since woods vary so much, the only way to arrive at the best colour for your purposes is to experiment, trying different strengths of stain and varnish until you get the look you like. The more heavily figured areas tend to pick up more stain.

RUBBED-IN PAINT:

This gives a similar effect, especially if you use the off-white or greyish paints which people like for the bleached driftwood effect that they can impose on even the most gingery deal. The finish will not be so transparent, or quite so durable since stain penetrates deeper than paint even when the latter is rubbed into the grain. It is, however, a quick method of giving wood floors a cool, even look, and makes a very attractive background for stencilling.

DESIGNER IDEAS

"I get asked to do a painted floor from time to time, often by Americans. They seem to be more into slightly 'over the top' effects. I find it incredibly easy, like painting on a table – much easier than going up and down a ladder. The best thing to paint is a good old pine floor, cracks and all. Cracks are fine. What is important is to get off all the polish, stains and varnish – anything like that. The floor should be sanded over with a machine. I use oil colours and undercoat – it needs to be an oil-based paint because that is the only one which sinks into the wood. I would give it two coats of thin undercoat as a base, just enough to change the colour of the wood.

My inspiration for floor designs comes from historical examples: paintings, prints and sometimes from furniture. One floor I did was taken from the design on top of a Turkish box. The floor in my

own house is based on a marble one in an Italian palazzo. One should adapt any design to suit oneself. In a big room with lots of furniture you are best advised to go for a background colour – the floor doesn't want to be more important than the furniture. Looking at old pictures is a great help in evaluating this sort of thing. I usually use the natural colours of wood, stone and marble. My own floor scheme uses

marbled white squares set in a 3-D 'lattice' in shades of brown. The tawny sections are the original well-scraped floor boards.

I find it helps to think of a floor design as a painted carpet. It should be flat and decorative, but not too painterly. I start by finding the centre of the room, which is where the lines connecting the centre of the walls intersect. Then, depending on the pattern, I begin marking it out clearly

with a pencil. You need to measure accurately. Then I mix up my colours and get down on my hands and knees and off I go. I use artists' brushes for fine detail and a decorating brush (small size) for filling in. When it is for a client, you go on until it is finished, varnish and all, but in my own place I kept adding bits when I felt like it, varnishing it as I went along. Varnishing is a bit of a drag, but you have to do it to

prevent the paint being worn away – anything from three coats to ten, depending on how much time you have and how much wear the floor is going to get. From time to time, if the varnish seems worn, take everything out and clean the floor thoroughly and re-varnish. It should last for years and years. ''

The best looking floor designs for painting, combing, or marquetry-type staining, usually allude to traditional flooring – tiles, parquet or paving.

Their geometric shapes look solid and coherent, extending over a floor space. They can either be painted onto smooth sheets of ply, or directly onto the floor boards ignoring the cracks, in the manner of Graham Carr.

LEFT *Cheeky, simple but effective, Cressida Bell's bathroom ceiling decoration is taken from the ideal* ad hoc *subject – the shower rose.*

RIGHT *Thanks to Paul Czainskis' masterful technique, a tiny disjointed space is transformed by the superb graining on the door, a painted marquetry floor and illusory stonework.*

ABOVE *The painted cornice and stonework, or 'ashlar', is stippled through stencils with a traditional grainer's mix of powder colour and stale beer.*

Preparation

The floor should be thoroughly scrubbed first with a de-greasing agent and left to dry. If this raises the grain too much, sand it lightly to smooth it.

Method

Almost any paint will do for rubbing in: emulsion, flat white (see suppliers index), eggshell or gloss. Thin the paint a little to make it easier to apply. Tint with appropriate colours. It can be put on in whichever way you find easiest: brushed on and then rubbed off, or rubbed in with a rag. To encourage the paint to soak in, coat the wood, leave it for a few minutes and then start rubbing off. This finish will need to be sealed in with two or three coats of matt or eggshell varnish – ideally dead flat, clear varnish which does not yellow.

STENCILLING:

There are stencilled floors in England dating from the seventeenth century, simple designs often centred on the family coat of arms. Stencilling has always been one of the easiest ways of adding colour and pattern to any surface.

The most acceptable design is one based on a carpet – with a border enclosing a central area stencilled on a regular grid. If this seems too ambitious, confine your stencils to a border around the edge of the floor and stain or paint the centre a solid colour. A neutral background, such as the rubbed-in finish, is very pretty stencilled in one colour – deep blue or burnt red, for example. The same colour and pattern can be repeated in a border on the walls.

Stencilled floors follow the same procedure as walls (see p. 94), but it makes sense to go for a tough paint. Signwriters' paints are good. Lyn Le Grice uses spray paints, which saves effort, but they can be tricky to handle as the paint often clogs up when the can is pointed downwards, and the colour tends to creep when it is sprayed at an angle. When spraying a border the skirting will need to be masked off, or re-painted later.

Thorough varnishing is essential, to prevent your work of art being rubbed away under passing feet. Depending on the colours, use flat, clear varnish, or a tough polyurethane, and give the floor several coats. Drying time is speeded if you leave a fan heater in the room, or the windows open in warm weather.

CHEQUERED PATTERNS:

Chequered patterns are the poor man's version of marble paving – at least if you tackle it yourself. Black and white lozenges painted over a plank floor in a hallway can look surprisingly convincing even though the floorboards may be gappy, and the painting quite casually done. Setting the chequers on the diagonal makes a hall look wider. In an old house the dim, matt effect of a non-shiny paint looks right, but for a crisper look substitute gloss and a shiny coat of varnish.

Method

Geometric patterns like these need accurate measuring. Mark off a long batten with your chequer intervals and use a smaller one, also marked off, to measure off the space between. No old floor is ever precisely square or rectangular with parallel sides. A solid-colour border, which can expand and contract to follow the walls, is the obvious solution. A magic marker gives clear outlines within which to paint.

For a black and white chequered effect, the whole floor should first be painted white. It does not have to be gloss; white emulsion will do provided you varnish it thickly at the end. Whatever colour combination you choose, paint the floor first with the lighter colour, then mark out the squares or lozenges, painting these with a pointed brush to outline the edges and a thicker brush to fill in the squares.

If you want to marble your squares see our section on marbling techniques (p. 68). If you are nervous of boldly dashing in veins, try Sally Kenny's playful ways of cheating to create a marbled effect (p. 166).

CEILINGS

COLOURWASHING:

The matt dapple of colour which colourwashing gives is very effective on ceilings. The Georgians and Victorians routinely coloured ceilings a couple of tones paler than the wall colour, a simple device which ties a room together without drawing attention to itself. If the walls have a brushy colourwash, the ceiling can be brushy to match (see p. 86 for colourwashing instructions). If the wall finish is discreet, you may want a softer ceiling look, which you can achieve by using two brushes – a wide paint brush to apply colour and a dry soft brush like the Whistler Lilyduster to soften out brushmarks while wet. To soften, move the bristles gently to and fro at right angles to the wet painted surface, teasing out the colour finely.

Limewashed ceilings were commonplace until World War II because apart from being cheap, limewash was considered hygienic, an antiseptic which also repelled insects. But as anyone who has restored an old house will know, old limewash has to be scraped or scrubbed off before any modern emulsion paint will adhere to a surface. So it is good to know that a newly available paint, called Keim after its German inventor, allows you to re-paint over a limewashed or distempered base. Keim paint is available, by post, in three formulations (see suppliers index). It is more expensive than the standard DIY paint but the manufacturers claim it provides a permanent finish.

Alternatively, if you live in an old, listed building you may again find the Society for Protection of Ancient Buildings can help you to locate actual limewash or distemper for restoration purposes.

STENCILLING:

If cornices are missing in an old house, it is a good idea to create some sort of visual replacement. Decorated walls which stop short abruptly when they hit the ceiling look unfinished. One solution is to stencil a border round the top of the walls, and then repeat the stencil round the ceiling, colourwashing the centre space in some pale shade keyed to the border colours or the wall colour. This is something I plan to do in my blue-painted study when I can escape from the typewriter, repeating the stencilled Indian motif border that goes round the walls. At present the white ceiling looks too much like a lid – unrelated to the room. Stencilling on a ceiling is done exactly as on any other surface, but is a little more back-breaking. Another cornice substitute has worked quite successfully in a spare bedroom and is less cruel to bad backs. A contrasting line is painted round the top of the wall. This line is echoed by a second line on the ceiling, set roughly where a cornice would reach to, and the centre space is colourwashed. The plain white area between the two painted lines becomes a 'negative' cornice.

One good reason for hanging upside down with a stencil brush is that a little decorative flair on a ceiling has great impact on our unaccustomed eyes, and makes an ordinary room re-

LEFT *Handled with conviction, painted architecture together with a cloudy marbled finish gives a strangely shaped space an ordered, framed appearance.*

ABOVE *How to handle a painted moulding when it goes round a curved corner – positively and crisply.*

markable. A wreath of stencilled roses would transform a bedroom into a boudoir, while a severe architectural frieze would lend great dignity to a hallway or study. The style to aim for here is Puginesque – consult paintings of the period for ideas.

SKY CEILINGS :

The idea of painting ceilings to look like a blue sky, complete with drifting clouds, dates back to classical times; it is a decorative conceit everyone can respond to. 'Sky' ceilings are currently popular because they create an airy, romantic canopy for rooms that need a bit of interest aloft without going as far as *putti* and garlands. I have seen them in hallways and dining-rooms, and they look particularly attractive in high-styled bedrooms. Nemone Burgess recently painted one in her bathroom, only there the 'sky' starts halfway down the walls and dissolves the contours of the small room so that you seem to be looking up into luminous blue space. More often the sky is framed by a cornice and confined to the ceiling. No great artistry is needed to suggest a sky convincingly in paint but it is hard work painting overhead. Most painters try to rig up portable scaffolding – boards stretched between two ladders – so they can paint while lying on their backs.

Nemone Burgess paints skies over a creamy yellow base coat: 'This gives a lit-up look, like sunlight.' She uses a surprising range of colours – cobalt, ultramarine and cerulean blue, but also Paynes grey, orange and purple. She mixes them up with a little proprietary glaze, and quite a lot of white spirit: 'too much glaze can turn blues turquoise.' She describes her painting technique as 'rather like marbling overhead – I go zing-zing across the ceiling with my colour onto a dry paint surface, and then I stipple it out until it looks soft.'

Having blocked in her sky and cloud shapes quickly and loosely with the overhead marbling, she then works up the ceiling a section at a time, adding more colour, stippling and softening, and standing back frequently to gauge progress.

Sally Kenny uses fewer colours over a white base – eggshell or vinyl silk. 'I'll use blue and white, of course, and greys and purple and maybe a little green. I brush the colours on in the ordinary way and then stipple over the colour, especially where two colours meet, so they seem to merge imperceptibly. When the paint is dry, I go all over it again with blue and white to bring it up where it needs dramatizing.'

Their skies are painterly, full of atmospheric effects, but a sky ceiling can work very well at a simplified level. Keep your cloud a skein rather than fat, nursery-rhyme puffs, and stipple out hard edges and colour demarcations. Do it in two stages, like Sally Kenny, to allow yourself time to ponder the overall effect. Then add white highlights, deeper blue depths, grey or green shading, and stipple again until merged. For reminders about cloudy skies, look at paintings by Constable, Claude Lorraine and Turner.

WOODWORK
FAKE MARQUETRY :

Cabinetmaker's marquetry consists of a decorative jigsaw of attractively grained wood veneers, cut and glued to a plain timber carcass to create patterns ranging from simple geometrics to the lavish rococo curlicues and floral motifs seen on seventeenth- and eighteenth-century Dutch pieces. On floors, the harder-wearing equivalent was parquet, *parquet de Versailles* being the most lavish with its use of precious woods and intricacy of pattern. Recently, many painters have been commissioned to paint 'fake' wood floors in patterns somewhere between elaborate marquetry and geometric parquet. Whole new floors of Canadian oak have been laid with invisible joins for the purpose. But common plank floors in reasonable condition look excellent given the same treatment, even when the cracks do show.

Fake marquetry is surprisingly easy to do and it dresses up small floor areas handsomely. Well-varnished and waxed, they last a long time, becoming weathered rather than worn-looking.

Preparation

Spend some time preparing the floor. Remove old tacks, hammer in loose nails and then sand over the boards to get a smooth, clean surface. A manual sander or power sander will do the job well – large machines can now be hired easily. After sanding, vacuum to remove as much dust as possible. Any noticeable holes can then be filled with toning plastic wood.

Method

Depending on the pattern you have chosen, you can either measure out the floor and pencil in the design, or make a template to draw round. When the shapes are clearly marked out, go over them with a sharp Stanley knife, cutting the outlines into the wood to a depth of about 3mm. This is to prevent colour seeping over the boundaries. Use spirit-based wood stains (see suppliers index) to colour in the marquetry. These come in a wide range of colours: light oak or teak, mahogany, Tudor dark oak, or black would give three nicely contrasting tones. Use a pointed brush for the outlines and fill in the rest with a painters' 25mm brush or a rag. Stain all the pieces of one colour first before going on to the next. Stains are best put on in the direction of the grain. If they dry patchily, go over them again.

Leave the floor for a day or two to dry, then vacuum again carefully to remove dust and hairs and give it three coats of eggshell or gloss polyurethane varnish. Begin varnishing in the corner farthest from the door. Thin the first coat with white spirit – about 3 parts varnish to 2 parts spirit – but thin the following coats less. If you sand the second coat of varnish, going with the grain and not rubbing too hard, and then wipe it over, your third coat will feel much silkier. Three coats of varnish is the minimum, and this is adequate on a small floor which does not get tramped over with muddy boots. Graham Carr has given a floor as many as ten coats of varnish. A spray attachment which will take varnish would make this job a lot easier, if available.

LIMED OAK GRAINING :

The neutral but textured look of 'limed oak' is a finish currently much in demand, according to virtuoso grainer Len Pardon. Details of his technique follow for you to try.

Preparation

The wood should be prepared as for marbling, with a white eggshell finish. You will also need steel combs (medium and fine), a sable brush and some rags.

Method

The colour Len uses is made from more or less equal quantities of raw umber, ivory black and Vandyke brown plus about half the total quantity of the other three in burnt umber (that is, 1 part each of the first three to $1\frac{1}{2}$ parts burnt umber). Mix them together with the glaze to make a deepish putty colour. Try it out on a white card to check.

A few painted lines can make all the difference to simply coloured walls. We took this idea from an old Swedish house, and painted the lines – not too precisely – in gouache colour 'fixed' with a little PVA adhesive.

Painted grisaille *cartouches, suggestive of carved ornament on French* boiseries, *add interest and prettiness. Here, they also have a practical function concealing a doorway.*

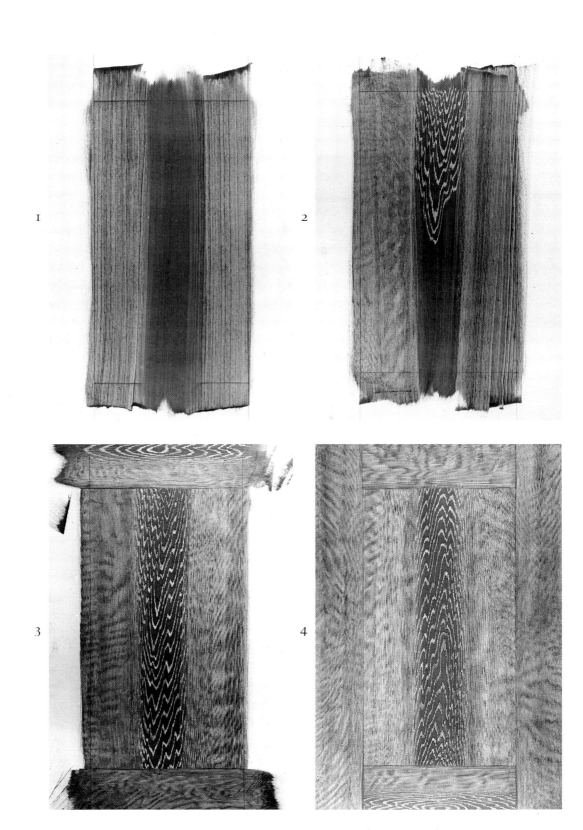

1 *Glaze brushed and combed over a door panel.*

2 *Heartwood being added in the central strip.*

3 *Liming colour applied and rag-combed over the horizontals.*

4 *Vertical stiles brushed and combed as before.*

5 *Completed door with quarterings and more heartwood.*

*One of the prettiest examples of fake panels. Silk-ribbon
blues in two tones, dragged and outlined in grey and off-
white, subdivide a flat wall.*

A dressier example of fake panelling, though no more difficult technically. Painted, distressed bands define and dramatize marbled walls in a tiny hallway.

Different ways of organizing surfaces by imposing painted panel shapes. Easiest to do are simple painted lines of varying thicknesses in watery colour. Alternatively, 3-D effects like traditional joinery can be created in monochrome. Dragged, combed or grained effects add texture and verisimilitude. 'Ashlar', or trompe stonework, is a matter of getting the shadows and highlights right, dovetailing where they meet.

Painted by Stephen Calloway, who taught himself to do these finishes, a marbled architrave and onyx-style decoration on the door panels look dramatic framed in black and white.

Lavishly marbled, a solid wooden architrave takes on new and palatial dimensions.

Paint the door panel by panel or, if it is a long straight piece of wood like a skirting board, grain it section by section. Brush colour evenly over the panel. Stretch a rag tightly over the teeth of a steel comb and draw the wrapped comb, with even pressure, down both sides of the panel, leaving approximately 75mm of darker colour down the middle. Then, using combs without a rag, comb at a slight angle over the rag-combed area, first with a medium, then with a fine comb. Leave the strip down the middle. Using the pointed end of the sable brush, scratch typical oak sap markings in the dark strip of glaze. Hold the brush as if you were drawing or shading. Sapwood has zigzag markings – look at a real piece for guidance.

Quartering, where ripple marks occur across the grain (again, study a real piece of oak), is done differently. Instead of leaving the dark strip, as previously, the whole panel is rag-combed, and then combed again with fine and medium combs, aiming at a clean-looking but slightly more rippled finish. Quartering is done with the sable and the same glaze, warmed a couple of tones with a touch of burnt sienna. Load the brush, but do not make it too wet. Stroke out the excess on a card, then pinch the sable to a chisel shape which lets the colour flow through. Starting at the top, draw out quartered shapes tapering down to a fine line, and then repeat this halfway across the panel. Quartered oak is cut across where the sapwood is formed, and it is the varying rate of growth which creates the fascinating shapes.

FAKE PANELS

Where I live in the East End of London, there are several streets lined with early eighteenth-century houses, whose main rooms are entirely encased in original pine panelling. The rooms have low ceilings for their size, which dip pleasantly here and there. The old panels are full of gaps and cracks but, with the shutters closed, lamps glowing and a fire in the hearth, it would be hard to imagine rooms more delightfully cosy to sit in. Yet for all their simplicity and their oddities, they are effortlessly elegant.

The 'woodiness' of the rooms (some are painted, some stripped) is part of their special charm, but I think the real clue to their effect is their consistent development of a classical notion of good proportion in an eighteenth-century idiom. The panelling is regularly subdivided, with a chair rail running round at approximately door-knob level, echoed by a sturdy wooden cornice above. The strong horizontals that these make are then challenged by the rectangles of the panels above and below the dado, which set up a rhythm just varied enough to be interesting. It may be a trick of the eye, owing to the different planes of the panelling, but all these rooms seem more spacious than they actually are.

To install real wood panelling today would, sadly, be beyond the means of most of us. The appearance of it, however, is so easily suggested with paint that I constantly wonder why more people do not investigate what can be done with a little texture and some elementary trompe l'œil.

It is quite astonishing the difference that even flat painted lines, arranged in panel-like sequences, can make. These fake panel treatments provide a visual framework to which furniture, pictures and so forth can be related. This is particularly helpful when you are trying to make sense of the usual odd assortment of furniture that you tend to start off with in the early stages of setting up home. As soon as these painted divisions appear on the walls, it becomes inevitable that a chest of drawers or a sofa stands centrally beneath and that pictures and lamps are disposed in a logical way to either side, or grouped above.

PAINTED LINES :

The simplest fake panel idea (see p. 132) is purely notional and consists of nothing more than coloured lines painted on the walls like large picture frames. This effect can be deliberately formal and symmetrical, but it would work just as well, I think, with a looser arrangement. The lines here – not mathematically precise, please note – have been painted on freehand with a watery colour. I used gouache with a little PVA binder to prevent trickles, and two brushes: a pointed sable for outlining (you should lightly pencil in outlines beforehand), and a filbert for filling in.

FAKE PANELS WITH STENCILLED OUTLINES :

This effect can look traditionally folksy, or, in sophisticated colours like a dirty grey-green with sepia-coloured stencils, move up market. The 'panels' could be dragged with paint a couple of tones darker than the background colour of the walls, which would be enough to differentiate them. Their shape could be emphasized by a tidy frame of pointed leaves, as exemplified in a design by Graham Carr.

PAINTED PANELS :

The blue showroom at Colefax and Fowler's London offices (see p. 136), looks charming and intimate. This is partly due to the very successful colouring of pale subdued blues, and partly to the straightforwardly painted 'panels'. They give this small, irregularly shaped room character and warmth. Note once again how using darker tones of paint on the panels (which are dragged, as is the background) suggests the varied planes of wood panelling. The three-dimensional effect has been strengthened by adding two paler lines around two sides of each 'panel' and two darker lines round the other two sides. This minimal effect is enough to indicate light and shade, and relief. The dragging is done in the way John Fowler liked it, with a confident brushiness that looks spontaneous and lively in the best hand-painted tradition. If you want your drag painting to look classy, this, rather than the mechanical perfection of printed imitations, is the look to aim for.

False panels need not imitate woodwork. In a small but choice hallway (see p. 137), finished with a subdued, painterly marbling, the lines that dramatize and define the space are brushed on in a deliberately uneven fashion, suggestive of marble inlay, but not too seriously. Note how the effect is carried across the radiator below the shelf. The effect of the larger 'panels', with their curved corners, has a look of lighthearted romanticism without pretentiousness – the essence of John Fowler's style.

6

RESTORATION, DISGUISE,
PAINTING FURNITURE
AND TRANSFORMATION

Painted furniture is presently enjoying a general resurgence of popularity. People are finding that painted pieces fit especially well in the colour- and texture-conscious interiors of today. Paint is also the perfect camouflage for less distinguished furniture – either what the professionals call 'brown' (anything wooden but not antique) or all those purpose-made items in modern materials, which can be turned out cheaply and do not merit a second glance as they stand.

The term 'painted furniture' is vague enough to include anything from a valuable old chest with original painted decoration, to the tawdry pastel-and-gilt bedroom suites still produced for large department stores, or a bedside table or odd chair on which someone has slapped a coat of pink gloss paint. Once your 'eye' is in, it is not difficult to distinguish good from bad. Painted furniture is always worth another look – if it is of period shape and newly-painted, the paint may have been added to smarten up the original paintwork beneath, which can often be uncovered and re-touched.

One of Alex Galitzine's stencilled pieces, a simple old chest
decorated with borders and posies in subdued 'old'
colours. Above it, a rosemaling hatbox, painted in
traditional colours by Ginty Watson.

Buying new painted furniture is expensive because of the man-hours taken to produce a well finished piece. It is a different story if you paint your own. Unless you cost your time, your hand-painted pieces will seem a remarkable bargain. And they can be worked at whenever you feel in the mood – which is not usually the case with a room. It is the ideal way to cut your teeth on the whole business of decorative painting; experimentation is easier, and the smaller scale makes the project less daunting and less tiring.

Restoration

Assuming it is solid and in good repair, a typical piece of 'brown' may only need to have the old finish removed to give a clean surface for paint. It is usually worth having furniture repaired professionally as it is exasperating to lavish time on making a piece look attractive if it functions badly.

If you find crude modern paint concealing an interesting old finish (this usually comes to light in chips and cracks), go carefully. I know someone who started work on a cupboard only to discover that she was rubbing off an original Burne-Jones painting with her wire wool. But modest pieces are often enhanced if you can uncover the original finish. I have been reasonably successful using paint stripper, wiping it away carefully with rags and using it on a small area at a time. Sally Kenny recommends acetone, or nail polish remover. It depends on the type of paint and varnish used originally. Sometimes it is only possible to salvage the hard, smooth priming – gesso in many cases – which painted pieces were given in previous centuries.

Painted detail can be put back – study any surviving decoration carefully first. Unless you are very sure of your brushwork, apply an isolating layer of white shellac – known as white polish – all over. This means you can wipe off

mistakes and experiment safely. Make sure it is bleached shellac rather than orange shellac or button polish. These have orange tones that will alter any existing colours. For retouching use a slightly transparent paint (basic glaze with more undercoat and matt varnish than usual) and if in doubt, keep colours muted.

Transformation and disguise

Decorative painting really comes into its own as a means of disguising those useful but uninspiring pieces of furniture. Do not paint mahogany or any fine wood of good colour and markings. Oak is better stained and filled (see limed oak, p. 174) as its open grain looks wrong painted. Paint soft-woods, and those spray-lacquered, knotty pieces of deal which look so sparkling when new but turn grey and sad with use. You can also paint kitchen and bathroom fittings or built-in cupboards.

Painted decoration should blend with your existing room. On the whole, special effects should be reserved for furniture that is attractive and interesting enough to play a star role; the best approach with yards of built-in cupboard doors might be to tone them in with the predominant room colour, perhaps breaking up the flatness with a lightly painted 'bamboo' moulding, or a plain line trim. You can have fun painting pieces with carved mouldings or decoration, barley-sugar pilasters, fretwork or knobs; or anything so plain that it can take a chic modern lacquer look, like spatter, for interest.

Preparation, Tools and Materials

The real craft of furniture painting lies in the preparation. While it may be sufficient for walls to look pretty, painted furniture is going to be used and needs to wear and handle well. If you have little time to spend on a piece but must have good results, your best bet is to give it two coats of undercoat tinted grey, dusty cream or snuff colour, and rub the paint down when dry so that the wood just shows through here and there. This way it will look old and worn, rather than the result of a skimped paint job – but it will not last very long.

Strip off any varnish using paint stripper and wire wool (use meths to remove French polish). Old paint need only be stripped if it is badly chipped or wrinkled. Otherwise simply rub the old paint back until smooth with the usual series of coarse, medium and fine grade abrasive papers. On bare wood – old or new – the first coat should be primer; on existing paint it can be undercoat. Any major filling should be done after priming as the primer highlights defects. The raw edges often found on built-in cupboard doors are best filled with a very tough substance such as car body filler and then sanded back until they are hard and smooth. Coarse grain may need overall filling for a really good finish. This is best done with gesso – traditional or acrylic (see p. 78). Professionals brush a coat of shellac, which is fast drying (an hour or less), over the filled and primed surfaces to seal them and stop the next layers of undercoat soaking into the porous filler.

The usual order of events for painting furniture is first primer, then undercoat, two coats of eggshell or flat oil paint, the decoration layer and two more coats of varnish. You should take it as axiomatic that every succeeding coat of paint or varnish, with the exception of the actual decorative ones, is better for being rubbed down. As the finish becomes smoother, the abrasive paper should be finer. On the last coats most professionals use papers lubricated with water (wet-and-dry) or soap to prevent scratching. Faithfully done, this sort of rubbing down produces a hard, smooth, thin but tough finish. A Colefax piece would probably undergo seventeen separate processes before completion, but no-one is obliged to take such pains. It is, however, worth taking

some trouble over small, much-handled pieces like boxes or trays.

Since many thin coats produce a better finish than fewer thicker ones, professionals tend to thin most paints and varnishes down a little. Three parts paint or varnish to one part solvent would be about right. Brush with the grain for one coat and across it for the next to prevent brushmarks piling up. If the piece can be worked on in a dust-free environment, you will save time removing grit, dust, hairs and other fall-out which sticks to drying surfaces. You could always make a temporary tent from plastic sheeting.

It also saves time to keep certain brushes for certain jobs: an old brush for primer, a couple of standard brushes in small and medium sizes for undercoat and paint, and a couple of fine-bristled varnish brushes for putting on varnish and shellac. Keep the shellac brush separate and clean it with meths. You will want to add to these for specific tasks: hogs'-hair stencil brushes, a swordliner or lining fitch, a dust brush for dusting and softening, assorted artists' brushes (pointed, filbert or square) for painting different strokes or marks. Other useful tools might include a metal straight-edge knife, a craft knife with square blades, masking tape, lots of disposable foil containers for mixing colours, plus lidded jars for storing surplus glaze. You will also need a supply of lint-free rags.

Paints

As outlined above, for almost all furniture painting you will need primer, oil-based undercoat and varnish. The undercoat can double as top coat when tinted, but a flat white or mid-sheen paint, preferably oil-based, gives a more luxurious finish. Gloss paint is never used in polite circles on furniture except on nursery pieces, and even there it is better to built up a gloss with varnish on top of a mid-sheen or flat paint. If you find exactly

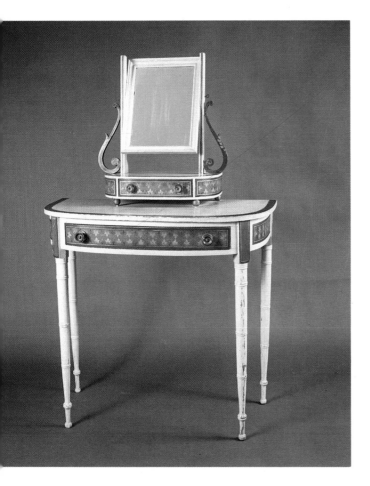

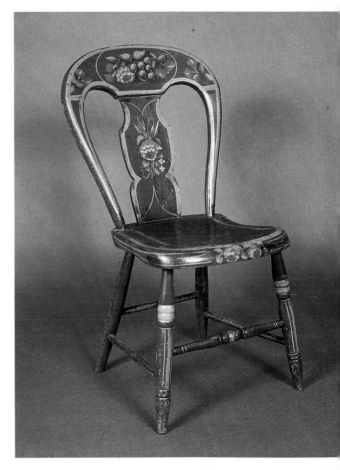

LEFT *An American, nineteenth-century dressing table set. The pale grey base contrasts with the red panels, lined and stencilled in gold in a style reminiscent of Hitchcock's chair decorations.*

RIGHT *One of a set of six, this richly decorated chair is dated 1820. Its croting and lavish yellow stripes bear a strong resemblance to the floral motifs of rosemaling pieces.*

LEFT ABOVE *Dated 1785, a Pennsylvanian dower chest painted with favourite folk motifs – hearts, tulips and vases – in traditional folk colours of red on blue.*

LEFT BELOW *Wonderfully vigorous and vivid, American folk graining at its best. The rope shapes are putty-grained in red with black loops on a white ground – proof that decoration can be technically easy but very stylish.*

the colour you want in a commercial range, buy that, but most professionals stock up on white paint and tint up their colours from these for each job. For dark colours, start with a commercial colour close to the shade, and modify with stainers or artists' oils.

Orange shellac and white polish are essential. There are various commercial glaze products, any one of which would do for furniture painting, or you can make up your own (see p. 47). Dead flat, extra pale varnish is very useful for adding to glazes as well as finishing non-shiny pieces. You will also need a gloss varnish. Clear polyurethane is easily available and quite tough; for really hardwearing surfaces use yacht varnish. Varnishes from the same product range can be intermixed to get just the degree of shine you want.

The above represents a basic paint kit for most purposes. Anything required specifically for a particular finish will be listed under that heading. Two other paints that you might find useful are red oxide metal primer (this is a cheap, handsome brown-red, which must be varnished to seal its 'tender' texture) and matt blackboard paint. This makes a useful black base but, like the red oxide, needs varnishing or waxing to give a surface – add a little brown or blue tint to the varnish to make the black more interesting.

Gesso

Gesso has been used for centuries to prime panels and to build up a flawless surface on furniture that is to be painted. In effect a surface primed with gesso has been covered with a very hard, fine skin of plaster. Despite the fact that preparing gesso is a bother, and handling it requires practice and judgement, the traditional form is still used in places like the Colefax and Fowler studio for fleshing out the ply and softwood used to make many small occasional pieces (see p. 78 for full details on making gesso).

For the amateur having fun with a few pieces, there is an effective modern substitute – acrylic gesso. This dries swiftly and needs no heating or mixing. It can be rubbed down to produce a surface almost as hard and uniform in texture as traditional gesso. But the old fashioned sort works out a lot cheaper.

Use a wide, thin varnishing brush to apply gesso. Six coats will build up a perfectly smooth surface, but with practice you can reduce the number to four, and for furniture priming fewer still may be adequate. Gesso is excellent for filling the surface of any open-grained wood before painting – the sort of wood that shows through as a finely ridged or crackled texture under endless coats of paint. Use fine grades of sandpaper for smoothing off the gesso. A final ivory smoothness is achieved by rubbing it over firmly, in a steady circular movement, with a soft old piece of sheet wrung out in water and folded into a smooth pad. Keep the pressure even, and do not linger too long in one spot because this smoothing is actually dissolving the top layer of gesso and spreading it out evenly. Before painting over gesso with oil paints it should be sealed with a coat of diluted shellac. Bear in mind that you are working with a transparent colour that cannot be painted out, so either stick to a simple effect or be prepared to shellac and paint it over if it goes wrong. Another possibility is to tint the gesso itself with gouache or powder colour, and finish with wax. Gesso takes a fine burnish.

Acrylic gesso is painted on in exactly the same way, and rubbed with fine abrasive paper until smooth. When rubbing down edges which have been gessoed, go carefully because they will be brittle and could chip off. If this happens, use a standard filler to patch them.

Since gesso acts as a primer, you start painting on it (after the shellac) with undercoat, and then go on to the usual oil-based paints. A gessoed surface is magnificent to paint on.

PAINTED FINISHES

All the decorative finishes used on walls can be transferred to furniture and look very attractive. The method is the same, so I will merely suggest some combinations which always work and look good.

DRAGGING:

Dragging, which is both neat and fine, is a formal finish which suits elegant furniture. Dragging over white (preferably off-white) gives subdued pastels, while dragging one colour over another can create wonderfully vibrant or subtle final shades. Dragging should follow the grain of the wood itself, travelling lengthways across table tops and drawer fronts, down table legs and dividing on frames, as on a door. Use a varnish brush to drag furniture, and the usual glaze, though it may look better slightly thinner. You could try artist Owen Turville's suggestion of dragging Plaka water paints, possibly adding Plaka medium for thickening. The only trim a dragged piece needs is lining – a thick and thin combination looks best – around drawer fronts, on table tops and so on.

STIPPLING:

Stippling gives furniture the same rich velvety bloom as it does walls. It is subtle, almost invisible except in close-up, but it makes a distinct overall contribution. Almost any strong dark colour on furniture looks better stippled. I also like it as a background to stencilling, tightened up with contrasting lines, or wide lines in the same colour. Stippling in a good colour will give any tacky furniture, provided you prepare it nicely, a new look of elegance.

SPONGING:

Sponging looks great in a strong colour, applied quite sparingly over a large, simple piece like a dresser or cupboard. It would be fun repeated over kitchen unit fronts too. In different colours, like peach and cream, tightly sponged prints could redeem every surface in a bathroom or bedroom. But please, if you have a decorative finish on the outside of cupboard doors, carry it over on the inside as well. Nothing looks meaner than opening a sleek, fancied-up door to be confronted with a bare blank inner face. Small details like these add a great deal of class.

SPATTERING:

Spattering on furniture is easier than on walls because you can take the item in question outside, where no masking off is needed. I find spattering goes nicely over sponging. If I want to finish a piece so that it tones with a room scheme or fabric using more than one colour, I might sponge it over fairly coarsely with the main colour. Then I would spatter on the others, plus a white or cream coat to soften, or a black one to sharpen it, until I liked the effect. The usual detail on this, too, is a lining trim, in the darker shade used. A spattered effect which suits spare modern pieces is achieved by pasting scraps of paper onto a dark base in a random fashion. The whole piece should then be spattered in toning colours. If you use dark grey as a base, spatter in granite colours – white, pale grey, black. When the paper is torn off, the shapes appear as abstract patterns. It looks very lively, especially when given a deep, ultra-smooth, lacquer type finish.

Build up abstract patterns by pasting torn paper onto a coloured painted ground, and then spattering in toning shades. Removing some scraps at different stages gives varying degrees of contrast.

DESIGNER IDEAS

66 Susan Williams used to run the Colefax and Fowler London studio with great verve, but she has since left to set up as a decorative painter on her own. Before her three and a half years at Colefax she did an art school training. A formidably competent young woman, and a perfectionist in her own line, she understands the complexities of her trade thoroughly – the sort of colour a client has in mind when they talk about a sharp yellow, how much 'lining' a piece can take and what paint to use, whether graining would look better done in oil or watercolour, how to achieve a good effect quickly. She is, in other words, that rare breed – a highly-trained, experienced and unflappable craftsperson.

Furniture painting and decorating at Susan's level tends to be a slow business, with most of the time being spent on preparation. Ten separate processes go into a standard, run-of-the-mill piece, but as many as seventeen may be necessary on a special item. A typical piece might start with primer, followed by gesso and filling. Then it will be rubbed down and given a coat of white polish, followed by undercoat and two coats of eggshell. A dragged glaze finish might be used together with any special decorating effects, followed by a thin coat of varnish. Finally, contrast lining might be added and then probably more varnish, a final smooth-over and perhaps a coat of wax.

A Colefax training encourages intelligent experimentation, and Susan has scores of less orthodox solutions tucked under that smooth head-girl appearance. For instance: 'If you are in a hurry with a piece, it is sometimes better to go for an effect which looks like a once-good finish that is now somewhat battered. A nice effect for some old wooden pieces simulates ebonizing, worn away at the edges and on the moulding. You just apply a couple of coats of matt black paint, and then wax the piece with fine steel wool, rubbing it down to the wood here and there, achieving a good sheen all over.' In the same spirit she suggests lining with a gold felt-tip pen. 'You can cut the tip with a scalpel to the shape you want. It doesn't look like real gold, but it makes a decorative effect and it is quite tough. I would just wax it over to protect it.'

Much of her decorative work is done with Liquitex acrylic colours, a technique she learnt at Colefax. 'You can get pearly colours with watercolour paints which you don't find with oils.' She

has used these for graining very grand bookcases in a burr maple finish, for dragging false panels in a soft terracotta, on furniture, and small knick-knacks. Adding acrylic medium, she says, delays drying long enough to create a distressed finish, providing you work fast. One discovery of Susan's is Dulux Weathershield, which she finds a very satisfactory paint to work with indoors. It has a fresco-like texture when thinned down, and is not gritty like many exterior paints. For graining she sometimes uses three worn-down brushes stuck to a piece of cardboard with masking tape. This gives an effect that is not too regular, or – a bogey word at Colefax – 'mechanical'.

She never has trouble mixing or matching colours, to which I can testify having watched her repeat a chintz fabric motif down to the slightest nuance of shading on a pair of painted lamp bases. She gave me the formula of the famous Colefax sharp yellow without even a pause for thought: a stock yellow undercoat, followed by a glaze of lemon chrome, raw sienna, raw umber and black. Raw umber and a tiny amount of black are present in almost all the firm's famously appealing colours. 'That started with John Fowler, I think. He liked raw umber with everything, and a little bit of black goes in as a matter of course.'

When hiring new painters for the studio, she went for people with some craft enthusiasm, like patchwork, or drying flowers, rather than those with art school qualifications. 'It takes a special sort of person to be able to paint the same little flower-stand or table a dozen times in a row, listening to *The Archers* on the radio, and doing each one as well as the one before.'

Her training method was simply to paint an item once, as a demonstration, and then let the class loose on a piece – having first sealed the surface with varnish so that errors could be wiped off. 'A new painter might do the same piece five times or more – and still get it wiped off again at the end of it all. But it is really the only way to learn. Doing it for "real" teaches you more about the whole business of decorating furniture than practising away on a board.' **"**

LINING

Painting a decorative line trim on a painted surface in one swift economical movement is a difficult trick to master. The experts agree that the only way to become a proficient liner is to equip yourself with a lining fitch, or a sword-liner, and a suitable thinned paint (basic glaze) and just practise on a smooth prepared board until you gain confidence. The special brush enables you to take up enough paint on the long bristles to allow quite a long line to be painted without needing to re-charge the brush. Well-painted lines add definition and a certain pro-fessionalism to a painted piece. But for those who just want to smarten up a painted table-top or box there are easier ways of getting an effect that is almost as good. Sally Kenny has never been able to master the lining technique, so she has devised various dodges which she passes on to you:

1) With a steel rule or straight-edge and a sharp scalpel blade, score the paint surface – lightly but enough to show – with two parallel lines as far apart as the desired width of your line. Then draw your sword-liner along and you will find that the paint stays inside the 'tracks'.

2) Use a felt pen, in a suitable thickness, and a ruler. Once varnished over or shellacked, this will look fine to anyone but a hawk-eye from the Colefax studio.

3) To line in negative, buy a role of 'pin' striping used on car bodies, stick that down, paint as usual, then peel off at the end to reveal a slick line of base colour.

Lines usually look best painted in a slightly transparent paint, expecially if they are more than a couple of millimetres thick. A little matt varnish, or indeed any varnish, helps the colour to flow smoothly. Alternatively, you could try the egg tempera mixture used by Leonard Lassalle (see p. 111).

VINEGAR GRAINING

Although you can use vinegar to imitate genuine wood grains of the bolder sort – oyster walnut, for example – it has a life of its own once you get started, and the random effects that can be made with a mere lump of putty are just as decorative. This is definitely a finish to have fun with, and can be used on a small-scale to enliven a bold, simple piece of furniture, or perhaps even on a large-scale for fake panelling. I vinegar-grained a cheap, self-assemble pine chair recently, and the transformation process took just three to four minutes' work. If you pay attention to the basic preparation, as I am always urging, and varnish carefully and well, your dresser, chest or chair will look like a collector's piece.

Colourways

The red oxide paint mentioned on p. 150 is ideal as a base colour for certain effects. A rich ochre yellow would look good too. Or, if you want to be different, black graining on grey would look dramatic.

Materials

To make the graining mixture, use powder pigments dissolved in standard malt vinegar, and add a little sugar (about 1 teaspoonful per $\frac{1}{2}$ litre) to help make it stick. The old provincial American grainers who used this domestic glaze tried all sorts of pattern-making tools – fans of pleated paper, dried corn cobs, crumpled paper and corks. You might like to experiment, too, but to start with the only other material you will need is a good lump of putty, kneaded and rolled into a cylinder for long, radiating shapes, or broken into stumps for stamping with.

Method

Dissolve your colour, vinegar and sugar together thoroughly. Try the mixture on a leg – it can be wiped off again easily with a damp cloth. The mixture will not coat the surface absolutely evenly, but it should more or less cover it. Once your mixture is right, brush it over one area of the piece at a time. Leave it to set for a minute or two, then begin making shapes with the putty. By stamping or rolling the surface, a wonderful variety of effects can be achieved, from complex spiralling shapes to seaweed-like blobs. Fan shapes can be created in the corners and circles in the middle of panels or drawers, with stamped shapes filling the spaces. It is one of those effects that should be spontaneous rather than laboured but try to take the shape of the piece into consideration. It only takes a minute to get the feel of this finish. As the graining mixture dries it will lose its sparkle, like a drying pebble. Do not worry – a coat of varnish or white polish will revive this at once.

ANTIQUING

Used in moderation, antiquing is a cunning device for dulling the brashness of new paint, softening decoration and ground colours into each other and suggesting something of the subtle patination that appears on a surface with time and use. The problem with this decorative trickery is that it is so quick and easy, and so immediately effective, that people do not always know when to stop as a quick look round the bedroom furnishing section of any large store will show you. Scrubbing burnt sienna glaze over the mouldings and into the cracks of your ivory-painted suite, so that it looks as though it had been dipped in treacle, is not the look to aim for. Sublety is the watchword.

Method

You can begin with the actual colours used to decorate the piece. Adding a little raw umber to most colours gives that slightly dusty, shadowed effect which makes colours look old. If this is not enough, try sponging over the whole piece with a thin wash of raw umber acrylic colour. As well as taking the other colours down a tone or so, it will settle into surface paint as darker flecks, which look natural and old. If using acrylic as a wash over oil paints, you can rub the colour in quite hard, repeating the process until you get the degree of duskiness you want. Raw umber dulls without dirtying, but it gives a cooler cast. For a warmer tone use burnt sienna in the same way, or a mixture of burnt sienna and raw umber. A spot of black can be tried too. But remember to use a light hand, and try the effect on the back of the piece or a leg until you are sure you have got it right. A final dodge is the addition of a little colour to the last coats of varnish, which thus become final layers of tinted transparent paint. Again, do not over-do it – the piece must not look *dirty*. Then gently rub down the second coat with wet-and-dry paper or fine steel wool to thin it here and there, which gives the surface a more natural appearance.

These are fast ways of cheating at an aged look. The slower, more controllable method is to mix up a glaze with raw umber and maybe a dot of burnt sienna. Brush this on, leave it for a few minutes until it is just beginning to set up, and then go over it with a rag, rubbing it away harder on the raised areas and the centre of panels and leaving more in cracks, carvings, and wherever dust might have naturally accumulated. Leave this to dry, and then cover the whole piece with matt varnish.

Powdered pumice or rottenstone (obtainable from cabinetmakers' suppliers) can be mixed into an antiquing glaze, which then takes on a dusty sheen.

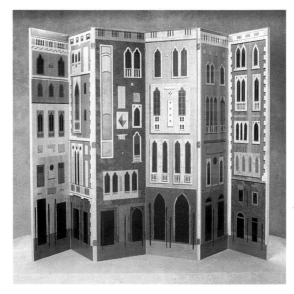

TOP LEFT *'Before', 'after' and 'in-between' – three views of a cheap but sturdy chair which was painted with red oxide metal primer, then vinegar-grained, varnished and waxed. A finish with great possibilities.*

ABOVE *Two different ways with a cheap mass-produced table; overall stencilling for a contemporary look, stencils in metallic powders on black for a more classic effect.*

TOP RIGHT *David Linley and Matthew Rice mix natural wood colours with carefully controlled stained veneers for their range of elegant marquetry pieces inspired by Venetian vignettes.*

ABOVE *Using ferns as templates, and stippling in*
near-black over bare blond wood, this magnificent effect
can be produced quite easily.

FRENCH POLISHING

French polishing was originally developed as a finish for high-class furniture made of wood. In skilled hands it brought up the colour and figurings beautifully, as well as creating a deep, flawless sheen. Though its skilled application is still chiefly reserved for fine wooden pieces, it has a useful role as a relatively fast but impressively professional finish on painted surfaces. It should not be used on table-tops, or areas which might get wet, because damp produces cloudy marks on the shellac. Essentially, the technique allows many successive coats of fast-drying shellac to be superimposed quickly, without brushmarks, the polish being rubbed on with a 'fadge' or rubber. When polishing painted pieces, use white polish because this will not alter the decorating colours.

Method

To make a fadge, take a section of cotton wool, pour polish onto it, wrap it in a square of linen – linen is lint-free – and press it onto a piece of board to distribute the polish and work off the excess. Then dab a little linseed oil onto the base of the fadge to prevent it sticking.

Spread the polish evenly over the entire surface of the piece, and keep the fadge moving the whole time. The movements for applying it are ritualized, so practise them mentally before starting. For the first coat of polish, cover the surface in overlapping circular strokes, sweeping on and off the surface at the start and finish. Immediately afterwards, go over the surface again with figure-of-eight strokes. The last coat uses straight strokes, travelling in the direction of the grain beneath. Leave this coat to set up for about half an hour. You should apply four or five coats, allowing the shellac to harden at intervals. The piece should then be left for a day or more to harden thoroughly.

The last thing to be done to a French-polished surface is to remove any traces of linseed oil. Do this by dabbing the fadge in methylated spirits, and then rubbing it in straight strokes over the polished surface. If the meths dries out, add more. After a few minutes repeat this 'spiriting off'. If you want a real mirror finish, a special burnishing agent can be rubbed on, and you should follow the maker's instructions. For a duller finish, rub over the whole surface with the finest grade of wire wool dipped in furniture wax. In both cases, the final task is to buff the surface with a soft lint-free cloth.

For rubbing down French-polished surfaces in between sessions, use silicon carbide paper in a very fine grade.

GILDING

Water gilding, that is, real gold leaf floated onto clay bole, is gold at its most radiant. It is not really for amateurs, however; if you want that quality of gilding you should take a course in the craft. The expert consensus seems to be that amateurs achieve the best effects using transfer leaf. Applying transfer leaf is straightforward. The clever part comes when you apply certain chemicals to it afterwards to tarnish, discolour or slightly pit the surface, which dulls its garishness, ages it, and makes it look altogether more convincing. The degree of discolouration is optional – if you watch the process, you can wash off the chemical when you reach an effect you like.

Materials

Transfer leaf comes in various colours: Dutch metal is the nearest to gold; there is also silver and aluminium. The fine metal leaves are backed by waxy paper. Scraps of leaf 'skewings' can be used for patching, or for decorative finishes (see p. 165). Gold size, used for sticking down the gilding, is like a yellowy shellac – buy the fast-drying variety. Gilding looks better if you apply it over a coloured base, imitating the traditional clay bole bases for water gilding – Venetian red for gold, blue for silver and yellow ochre for either.

Method

The paint surface should be as smooth as you can make it, whether we are talking about a picture frame, a small stencil to be applied to a table-top, or bands of gilding on a turned chair back. Brush size carefully, in a good light, over the areas where you want to stick the leaf. Fast-drying size is usually ready in an hour, but check the instructions and test by touching it lightly – it should be just tacky, not sticky or wet. Then, picking up a sheet of transfer leaf, press it leaf-side down onto the size and rub it firmly from the back with your fingers. When you peel off the waxy paper, the leaf will remain with shreds hanging off. Leave these for now, and carry on over all the sized areas. You need to work fast to catch the size before it gets too dry. Finally, smooth down the leaf with cotton wool, removing all loose shreds. Any bad 'skips' will need patching – if the size is already too dry, apply more.

'PATINATING' ON METAL LEAF :

Most of these chemicals come in crystal form, so be careful of splashes when mixing up. Wear rubber gloves to prevent staining, wash off spills and work in a well ventilated room. Sally Kenny suggests using these chemical compounds over metal leaf, silver particularly, to suggest age and create a more interesting surface.

To tarnish silver leaf use potassium permanganate mixed with distilled water. Potassium sulphate mixed with distilled water will tarnish silver to an opalescent finish. Copper nitrate mixed with ammonium chloride and distilled water in the

Two methods of applying gold through stencils. Transfer leaf is most easily applied over designs previously stencilled with a mixture of gold size and a little colour. Metal powders are more tidily applied through the stencil itself onto a previously sized base to prevent seeping.

Hand-painted fabric in the form of cushions. Owen
Turville painted all these with acrylic colours on calico or
silk, sizing the cloth first with dilute acrylic medium.
Some artists use Florentine, or Eliza Turck's fabric
painting medium.

Marbling in the exact tones of the wallpaper has made this
frame almost disappear.

This frame has been finished in porphyry spatter, while
the tulips have been painted in tempera colour onto silk
shantung in the style of nineteenth-century botanical
painters.

This was an octagon of plain ply before painter Mark Ram turned it into a chinoiserie fantasy with a finish like old lacquer.

Old penwork pieces are so decorative they are immensely sought after today. Materials are simple: pen and ink. I did this little box as a holiday task.

Crackleglaze produces a complex decorative finish, like craquelure on porcelain, or fine snakeskin. Plain tables can be transformed with this delicate finish.

ratio of 1 part water to ½ part each of the chemicals will give metals a greenish, pitted look. Brush on the chemical you have chosen, wait until you see the right degree of reaction, then remove the chemical by flooding the surface gently with more distilled water and gently wiping it with cotton wool.

STENCILLING

Stencilling is a simple, attractive way of dramatizing or personalizing a piece of painted furniture. Stencilling on furniture is done in exactly the same way as stencilling on walls, or floors (see pp. 94–111, 126). The only point to emphasize is that when done on a small scale it needs to be more crisply and meticulously finished. The creative challenge comes in finding (or making) stencils appropriate to a particular piece, and in working out colours and an arrangement of motifs which underline its character and shape.

Stencilling in the folk style inspired by the Early American school looks best on simple pieces with a rustic air – dressers, blanket boxes, kitchen bits and pieces, or furniture for a child's room. Pre-cut stencils in this style are quite widely available. One mistake that people sometimes make is to go for too many colours, an over-naturalistic approach. This can look twee and fussy. Many old stencilled pieces were in fact painted in a limited colour range on dark or sludgy background colours. It is the *shapes* the stencil creates that make the decorative impact. For a sense of how such motifs would have been used one cannot do better than look through books on folk art (see bibliography) or at actual examples, like the ones in the American Museum at Claverton Manor near Bath. Old stencil motifs often seem vulgarized in modern interpretations because shiny paint has been used. They look most attractive when painted with a dry-looking matt paint over a lightly distressed background colour.

Alex Galitzine is a professional stenciller and decorative painter who especially enjoys working on furniture. She is a self-taught painter, disproving the notion that special training is essential. The actual stencilling of a piece takes her next to no time, but she may spend days thinking out the design if she is not working to a deadline. Her painting idiosyncrasy is to use tiny Humbrol enamel colours, of which she has a huge stock, for all her decorative work. Her affection for these enamels first began when she used them to paint chinoiserie-style pieces. They come in matt and gloss forms, and with these she can get virtually any effect she wants.

As stencilling adapts itself to more sophisticated furniture, it usually becomes more abstract. You have only to compare the stylized tulips in Mary MacCarthy's marquetry stencils with a folksy basket of tulips to see what I mean. On the richly-coloured pieces designed by William Morris's workshop, or the Victorian architect William Burges, stencils play an important but subordinate role, creating dense areas of continuous pattern surrounding painted panels.

Stencils for this sort of continuous pattern will have to be made yourself. Textiles, old and new, are an obvious source of ideas. The design I stencilled on a cheap coffee table as a demonstration piece was taken from one of the Victoria and Albert Museum's many Indian fabric printing blocks. The table is stencilled in a very straightforward style in inky-blue onto a greyish-yellow (see p. 156). Acrylics are good for an awkward object like a table as they dry so fast that there is no risk of smudging as you turn it round or upside down. Felicity Binyon and Liz McFarlane swear by Keep's Intenso colours for sign-writers, which are also fast drying. Stencilled finishes like these are adaptable: they can be used as discreet elaboration on a handsomely-shaped piece, or, conversely, they can make a mass-produced item look well-behaved enough

for company, yet unobtrusive. You can break up the patterning with solid-coloured mouldings, or ovals and circles (on top of a table, for instance) outlined by a fine line in the same colour.

GILDED STENCILS

Stencilling in gold looks effective if you do not overdo it. It can be done with transfer gold leaf, or with metal powders, onto fast drying gold size. I find it helps to give the surfaces a coat of shellac or varnish before adding gold, especially in the case of powders which infiltrate everywhere.

Method

Stencil the shapes onto the piece with the size, which should be tinted first with oil colour – this will help you to see where you have stencilled. When it is just tacky, with the stencil in place as before, press down your sheets of transfer leaf and peel off the backing. Cut the sheets close to the size of your stencil if it is small, and overlap them if it is large. Dull the gaudiness of new, metallic leaf by shading areas with a burnt sienna tinted glaze or adding lines in Indian ink – or both.

Metal powders look pretty if you dapple their colours a little, adding copper or silver to gold or bronze. The effect is much softer than transfer leaf. Use something like the foam applicators sold with eyeshadows to pick up the powder and press it onto the gold size. Do not overload the applicator, go slowly and for goodness' sake don't sneeze. You may find it tidier to apply the metallic powders through the stencil cut-outs, pressing the card down to stop it seeping underneath. When you have powdered all the stencilled areas, leave it to set for an hour. Then carefully rub off anything that has settled on the varnished surface with a damp cloth. Metallic powder sticks very firmly over size. Tidy up edges with the original paint colour.

ABOVE *A small, all-over stencil taken from a fabric block, this can be built up to cover an entire piece (see p. 156).*

BELOW *Birds, flowers and butterflies – perennially popular stencil subjects, can be combined in all sorts of different ways.*

PENWORK

Penwork decoration can be done to great effect on quite a large scale as well as on small boxes, trays, frames, drawer fronts or inset panels and knick-knacks. On a large scale it is undoubtedly time consuming – it takes months to achieve some sensational effects – but the result might well be an heirloom. Sources for most of these black and white designs are traditionally engravings and pattern books of classical ornament, but the technique is open to all kinds of new interpretations.

Wood and metal are equally suitable surfaces to work on. A few coats of gesso (see p. 150) make an excellent base on both materials. Metal, however, should first be cleaned of all rust and given a coat of metal primer. The gesso should be sealed with white polish or orange shellac giving an ivory or straw-coloured base respectively.

The only equipment I use for penwork is indelible Indian ink and a selection of mapping pens, which give suitably fine lines. On a larger piece, pens with slightly broader nibs would be useful. Having chosen my design elements, for example a classical scene set in a decorative border (see p. 161), I rough it out on the surface (attempt one face of a box at a time) in fine pencil lines. Then I just leap in with my pen and ink, reproducing the original with a wealth of fine detail, shading and cross-hatching in the manner of old engravings. You may be a bit anxious at first about making mistakes, but practice soon makes for confidence. Mistakes can sometimes be very delicately wiped off with a cotton bud dipped in meths, or touched out with Tippex, but on the whole I think it looks better to try and incorporate them into the design. As one surface is completed, seal it with more white polish to protect it while you tackle the next. Lining is best done using Sally Kenny's easy method, that is, with scored 'tracks'.

For pieces which are liable to get wet, a clear eggshell varnish, applied with a varnish brush and rubbed down sensitively with wet-and-dry paper used with water, gives a very strong finish. Apply two coats of varnish before you begin rubbing down in case you cut back to the decoration.

SPECIAL EFFECTS (see pp. 168–9)

Sally Kenny is a young Australian decorative painter who started learning her trade early – her antique-dealer father asked her to 'have a go' at restoring pieces when she was still a child. Sally's boxes, shown here, are painted to show clients the range of her special effects. She spends many evenings happily experimenting on what were originally a job lot of crystallized fruit boxes. Marbling is her speciality and she stresses the importance of looking at real examples.

MALACHITE:

Materials

This is a very simple finish, though it may not look like it. The base is a commercial colour – Dulux Tourmaline Green – in a mid-sheen finish. The glaze is made up of 70% Ratcliffe Glaze tinted with viridian artists' oil colour (to which a speck of ultramarine and yellow ochre may be added for variety), and 30% white spirit. A little matt varnish will speed up the drying process.

Method

Coat the surface liberally with glaze and dab with a soft cotton cloth. Tear a piece of card from a Kleenex box or cereal carton and fold it, making a fuzzy, uneven edge along the fold line. Using this as a tool, bring it down gently in one corner of the surface and make characteristic malachite stripes, some straight and long, some round. Cover most of the area, making different-sized shapes. Spin a small, worn, stubby brush (No. 6) here and there to make small circles, and stipple in darker areas. Then soften the whole surface with a rag, radiating out from the centre and travelling in one direction to give movement to the shapes. When it has dried, apply varnish followed by French polish and then wax.

WALNUT :

Method

As for malachite, except that the finish is done with a brown glaze – burnt umber, black and a little burnt sienna – over a putty-coloured base. The shapes are defined with a piece of torn cardboard, and details are added in the same way as for malachite.

AGATE :

Method

Round a white centre, draw in lines with a thin, pointed brush in earth colours, ranging from raw sienna through burnt sienna to dark burnt umber and black. Agate shapes should never be left with ragged edges, but should be gently softened sideways at right angles to the striations. The white centre can have swirls spun with a stubby brush to represent crystallization.

ROSEWOOD GRAINING :

Method

Over a shell-pink eggshell base brush a smooth coat of glaze, tinted with burnt sienna, burnt umber and a touch of rose madder. Leave until the glaze is half-dry – just tacky enough to be moved by the brush – and then draw striped grain patterns across, dipping the brush tip into a mixture of burnt umber and black. The stripes will merge with the base paint as it dries. If you want a more tigerish effect, add black stripes when the first coat is dry. Finally, apply varnish, or French polish and wax.

NATIVE GOLD :

Method

A pale blue-grey base is dabbed with a variety of glaze colours – coral (made with white, lemon yellow and rose madder), pale green and light grey. Rag the glazes in order to soften the colours, and then let them dry. Paint the desired shapes in quick-drying gold size. Pick up crumpled scraps or 'skewings' of Dutch metal transfer leaf and dab them onto the wet size. Then pat flat with cotton wool. Using a little coloured varnish, vary the tones of the gold skewings, making some warm, some cool or dark. When dry, spatter all over with three tones of grey. The last coat of French polish can be spirited out and the surface burnished with steel wool.

RED AND GOLD :

Method

This finish must be done on a horizontal, level surface. The base should be a vivid poppy-red eggshell. The glaze (70% glaze to 30% white spirit) is tinted with vermillion, crimson and rose madder, and sponged on for a mottled effect. It should be softened slightly. Sprinkle copper, pale gold and silver metallic powders randomly into the wet glaze. Then, with a brush, drop a little white spirit carefully into the glaze. It will create roundels as it spreads. Emphasize with colour when the surface dries. Varnish and rub down.

LAPIS LAZULI :
Method

The ground should be gilded with Dutch metal transfer leaf. Mix up glazes in ultramarine, a little Indian red, mid-grey, raw sienna and white. Cover most of the ground with blue, leaving some vein-like areas. Then add white and grey veinings, some stippled white flecks and then soften a little. Add some well-thinned raw sienna, diluted copiously with white spirit so that it spreads gently. For variety, tap this on from a height. Let it dry, varnish it, and then apply French polish and burnish.

TORTOISESHELL :
Method

Using a sea sponge dab straw-coloured paint onto a white base to give a mottled effect. The colours Sally uses for markings are burnt umber, black, and burnt and raw sienna. She puts in the markings with a soft brush, beginning with the palest: largish patches of raw sienna, softened, are overlaid with warmer brown markings made with a little burnt sienna and burnt umber, overlapping some of the first patches. Soften. Over these still smaller markings are added in black mixed with burnt umber, keeping mostly within the previous patches. Some dark colour should be flicked on in the lighter areas. The whole surface is lightly softened to blur the shapes into each other, but not so much that the edges appear frayed. Sally created the white banding on her tortoiseshell box, which looks like ivory inlay, by sticking pin-striping straight onto the base coat before painting and finally French polishing the box. She then removed the striping, leaving a pale indented line. Polish once to seal.

BASIC SIENNA MARBLE :
Method

This finish has an orangey cast, 'like old clock faces'. It is painted on a white eggshell ground. Two tones of yellow are mixed, one using raw sienna and a touch of orange in basic glaze, the other cadmium and raw sienna, also in glaze. These colours are brushed on in irregular patches, leaving plenty of white showing. Pale mid-grey is applied here and there, and is then distinctly veined in a darker grey, the patches being outlined in the darkest tone using a sword-liner. This is then softened out. Using grey to black, add darker veins across or through the previous veins. Using dead white glaze and scrumpled tissue paper, dab lightly over the marbling; then soften.

For variants on basic sienna, Sally might change the colours, using very pale yellows with more pronounced black veining, or she might alter the marble formation itself, going for an angular zig-zag effect 'like fifties formica'. Some sienna contains only pale-grey and white, plus a lot of quartz.

For finishing marble Sally likes to coat it with matt or eggshell varnish, and then just before this is quite dry, she rubs in French chalk (or household flour) which soaks up any remaining tackiness and takes on a soft shine when polished.

Sally stresses that the best confidence booster for novices attempting these special effects is to study small bits and pieces on the natural materials themselves, collected either from junk markets or from specialist shops.

SNOWFLAKE OBSIDIAN IN NEGATIVE :
Method

This needs to be done on a level horizontal surface. The white base is rubbed over with a mixture of 3 parts linseed oil to 1 part siccative, or dryer. Mix up your colour – black plus raw umber – into a little of the same mixture until it reaches the consistency of single cream, and then drop it on here and there. In the middle of these drops place a tiny amount of white spirit with the tip of a brush, and tilt the box so that the mixture spreads out to form coral or sunflower shapes. This finish may take two days to dry, according to Sally. She sometimes uses spray varnish or re-touching varnish to speed up the drying process.

ROSEWOOD AND WALNUT CROSS-BANDING:

Method

Follow the method for malachite, but use a burnt umber or black glaze over a biscuit-coloured base.

Over any finish which might lift or seems fragile, Sally brushes on four coats of white shellac before moving onto the fadge and French polishing stages. In this way she can build up a good surface in a day.

ROSEMALING

Rosemaling is Norwegian for 'rose painting', a highly stylized and colourful floral decoration which seems to have originated in Scandinavia in the eighteenth century, spreading to Northern Europe and ultimately to the United States with the great wave of Scandinavian immigrants. Rosemaling is strongly regional in Norway, with different areas having their own characteristic colours and styles of execution: Telemark rose-maling is painted in an asymmetrical fashion with rococo 'croting' shapes – 'C's and 'S's – on a background of black, dark green or rusty red; Hallingdal rosemaling goes in for asymmetrical arrangements of roses in bold colours on a

Parisian-blue ground; and Westlandet goes for a more folksy effect on a red ground. Rosemaling is enjoying a revival in Norway today, and I was lucky enough to meet Ginty Watson, who studied

Rosemaling, like most folk decoration, is built up of brushstrokes, flicked on in one movement. Repeat the shapes shown here, over and over again, until the process is unthinking and easy. If you practise on a surface sealed with varnish, it can all be wiped off again.

The spotty 'dalmatian' of paint finishes, Sally Kenny's snowflake obsidian in negative.

Fantasy finishes like these are wonderful in the right place. Gold leaf 'skewings' and metallic powders build up a jewel-like intensity together with richly-coloured glazes.

Two ways with sienna, one vivid, the other refined, plus a purely fantasy finish in tones of grey.

Malachite and a fake pietra dura *marble mosaic.*

A chic trio in shades of tawny: oyster-walnut on top of tortoiseshell on top of blond graining.

A striking effect produced by scattering bronze powder onto wet glaze.

the different regional techniques while she was living in Norway. A well as painting our hatbox (see p. 144), she told me how rosemaling is done in Norway today and her techniques are noted here for you to try.

Materials

You will need sable brushes in various sizes. Oil colours can be used almost straight from the tube, though some colours might need a little mixing or perhaps a little white spirit in order to dilute them.

The items to be decorated should be sandpapered in the usual way to get a smooth surface. You should wipe the piece over with linseed oil before you start to enable the colours to flow more smoothly. You learn as you paint, according to Ginty. 'Always paint with one hand resting on the other for extra control.' You are not supposed to draw the design in first, but a chalk circle helps to keep the design symmetrical. Rosemaling is all in the brushstrokes; the only way to get them flowing properly is practice. The design looks like nothing at all until you add the 'croting' – the outlining which goes on after you have put in the basic roses and flowers and leaves. Usually this is done in a creamy-yellow colour – white with cadmium or ochre – but sometimes black is used. For the shaded leaves, take up two colours on the brush, lighter on one side, darker on the other, so they blend together as you brush in the shape. In a warm place, the painting should dry overnight. To finish off, give it a coat of clear varnish.

Ginty paints small pieces, mostly, though she has done chests-of-drawers and bedside cupboards. Much as she enjoys this type of folk painting as a hobby, she says she has to be careful not to put roses everywhere. 'One or two things in a room is enough, otherwise it begins to look ridiculous.'

FERNWORK

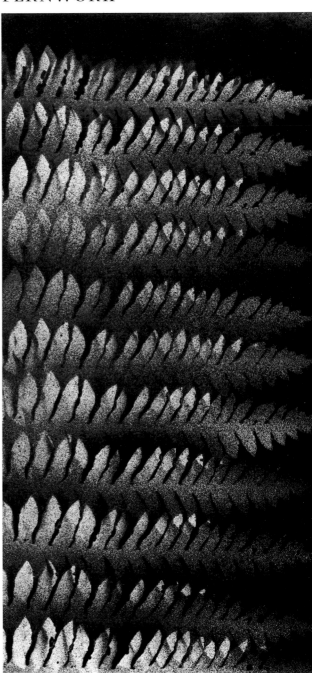

Moving a fern leaf along, and stippling, gives a leafy border like those on old papier maché trays.

FIREPLACES

Now that fireplaces, whose cheery blaze may well come from gas logs these days, have been re-instated as the natural focus of a room, people are looking for appropriate ways of re-vamping or rejuvenating fireplace surrounds. Overpainted marble or slate presents no problem that a quick coat of paint stripper cannot solve. But very often you are faced with something that is less adapt-able to contemporary decorating ideas – heavy-looking surrounds of varnished oak, excellent examples of period joinery but lacking in charm, or cast-iron surrounds smothered in old paint. Sometimes, too, you inherit a reproduction sur-round, installed during the pine-with-everything phase in the seventies, which suddenly looks oddly out of place. Provided the fireplaces in-clude the usual slips of marble, slate, iron or tiling round the grate (whose purpose is to resist the direct heat of the fire), wooden or iron surrounds can be given decorative finishes to make them fit in with updated colour schemes.

PORPHYRY:

A porphyry finish is much easier to do than it looks. It suits plain and chunky surrounds rather than fussy ones. Real porphyry is usually a rich dark claret to maroon colour – 'liver'-coloured – but the same spattering technique can be trans-posed to any strong colour successfully. I have seen it done with blues, greens and greys.

Method

The procedure with all the porphyry-type fin-ishes, whatever the colour, is to begin by spong-ing on a flat oil-based paint, tinted to a tone darker than the colour you eventually want, over a flat white base. The sponging should be quite even, giving a mottled effect. Spattering in vari-ous colours is the next stage, which gives the vivacity of polished stone. Before attempting this you should mask off the surrounding area with newspaper and masking tape – spatters are apt to spread. The first coat of spatter paint should be a cream, or off-white colour, made by tinting the same flat white with a little yellow ochre and/or raw umber, and then thinning it with white spirit until it is quite fluid. Spatter this evenly over the sponged colour, just enough to lighten it by a couple of tones overall. For a straightforward porphyry the next spatter coat should be black, thinned in the same way, and applied less heavily but evenly over the entire surface. If you want a more dramatic effect, you could spatter first with a related but contrasting colour to your base colour – crimson on red, turquoise on blue, emerald on green. Flick this over lightly, just enough to create a lift in the overall tone, and then move on to the black spatters.

Finish with two or three coats of clear gloss polyurethane varnish for protection. The varnish can be lightly tinted with oil-colour if you feel like heightening the tone of the finish. The second coat of varnish, and any further coats, should be rubbed down with fine wire wool, or wet-and-dry paper, to smooth and dull the surface just a little. Sally Kenny finishes her fireplaces with wax and finest grade wire wool.

STONE STIPPLING:

Less formal than porphyry, this is a useful way of softening and lightening a fireplace surround to blend in with a cool modern interior.

Method

Depending on whether you want your stone to look grey or yellow, start with a pale grey or sandy-coloured base, tinted with flat oil paint or vinyl silk. Make up a basic glaze, using undercoat but not proprietary glaze, tinted with burnt umber, a touch of yellow ochre and a dot of black.

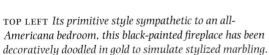

TOP LEFT *Its primitive style sympathetic to an all-Americana bedroom, this black-painted fireplace has been decoratively doodled in gold to simulate stylized marbling.*

BELOW LEFT *Cast iron can be picked out in contrasting paint colours, either richly pre-Raphaelite, or sweetly pastel, as here.*

TOP RIGHT *Taking its colour cue from the Fornasetti theme, a black and white fireplace – black, veined in white, for the pilasters, plain white gloss for the shelf on top.*

BELOW RIGHT *Inside a magnificent carved and gilded Portuguese frame, hand-painted Delft designs imitate old tiles. An idea that can be added to as time allows.*

*Sponged supports in sludgy colours frame a vivid little
landscape with figures in bright colours for a cottage-style
room.*

Paint it over the fireplace a section at a time, and while the glaze is wet pat it all over with a sponge to mottle it. Leave it to dry. Mix up a second batch of glaze, in a colder, stony shade, using Paynes grey and a little raw umber. This time use proprietary glaze instead of undercoat, and repeat the mottling process. When dry, varnish with two or three coats of eggshell or gloss clear varnish, but dull down the final coat with wet-and-dry paper or fine wire wool.

LIMING WITH WAX AND STAIN :

Oak, that problem wood that looks funereal when varnished and wonderful when blackened with age, is enjoying a revival. Our fashionable finish is an updated version of the limed effect produced in Vienna around the turn of the century by the Wiener Werkstätte, and later by firms like Heals in the twenties and thirties. Their solution to the coarse grain, characteristic of oak, was to fill it with a white paste filler. This did the double task of levelling the surface, so it could take a smooth polish, and turning the natural wood markings to decorative effect. The difference between the two approaches mentioned is that the Viennese stained the wood black first, against which the filler stands out dramatically, while the latter tended to bleach it so that the overall look was smoky-grey. Both look elegant and are good ways of re-styling varnished oak to fit in with current nostalgia.

Preparation

Your first task is to strip off the varnish, French polish or paint. Use paint stripper and scour with coarse wire wool until the wood is back to its natural biscuit shade. Then go over it in the direction of the grain with a wire brush. This opens up the grain markings to receive the filler.

Method

If you want the Viennese look, stain the oak with commercial black wood stain (Indian ink makes a plausible alternative). For the bleached version, use either an oxalic-based wood bleach (see suppliers index) or rub greyish-white paint into the wood. This is cheating, but gives much the same effect. When it has dried the wood should be sealed. This will prevent the liming sinking in anywhere except the scoured-out grain. Bleached shellac – often called white polish – does this quickly and efficiently. It is touch-dry in minutes, though it is best left for an hour or so to harden. When quite dry, apply the filler. Specialist stores sell a pasty white wax called liming wax for the purpose. This is simplicity itself to use. It should be rubbed on with a rag, first against the grain and then with the grain. Check to see that it has filled all the open grain markings. Polish it off with a soft cloth having allowed a little time for it to harden. The waxed finish can be lacquered or shellacked after overnight-drying to seal it and give the wood a sheen. This looks best on the bleached oak.

I prefer to fill black-stained wood with a standard filler, or gesso (see p. 150) diluted to a paint consistency and brushed on. Leave this for a few minutes, then wipe off firmly with a wet cloth, so that it remains only in the grain. This looks more dramatic on black wood because it dries very white. However, it must not be varnished or shellacked to seal it because that would make it transparent again. A light waxing is all it needs to protect it and seal in the stain, bringing it up to a dull shine.

It is worth experimenting with variants of this finish if you want to give oak furniture a new lease of life. The wood can be stained with colours other than black – dark green, red and grey, for example. But remember to seal it before liming so filler only enters the grain.

PICKING-OUT CAST IRON RELIEFS :

Victorian cast-iron fireplaces lend themselves ideally to the enjoyable game of picking-out their relief designs in various paint colours. Base your colour scheme on those richly coloured pieces of majolica or faience. Painted like this, a standard cast iron surround which you do not want to have sand-blasted (expensive if it has to be removed and then re-plastered in) becomes highly ornamental. It would look excellent in a room with a grandly printed wallpaper in the Morris style. Alternatively, in a simpler bedroom scheme, you could paint the surround in Wedgwood colours, chalky pastels with white (see my fireplace, p. 172).

Preparation

If the fireplace is already painted, and in reasonable shape, you need only fill in the chips with filler, apply a layer of undercoat and then paint as with any other surface. If, on the other hand, it is clotted with old paint, badly chipped and rusty, it might be better to remove the old paintwork. Mask off the wall, apply paint stripper with an old brush and then remove the softened paint with a scraper, coarse wire wool and a wire brush. Having cleaned it back to the metal, start by giving it a coat of anti-rust metal primer, then undercoat as above. Flat oil paint is a nice smooth paint for this sort of work (see suppliers index); otherwise use standard undercoat, tinted up, and varnish to seal.

Method

Mix your paint colours and apply them using pointed sable brushes for outlining the raised areas and a small standard brush or a filbert for filling in the background and larger areas. Var-nish darker colour schemes with eggshell polyurethane and pale ones with extra pale, dead flat varnish. You can add a little gloss to this if you want a shine, although you should remember that Wedgwood pottery has a matt surface.

CRACKLEGLAZE

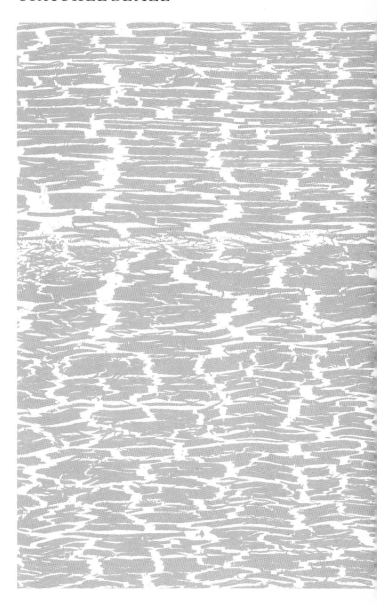

The effect of crackleglaze is dramatized when two strongly contrasting colours are used, black on white, red on black. There are various forms of special glazes; ours depends on using water-based paints. Alternatively, use pale colours to give a delicate porcelain finish (see p. 161).

7

THE GREAT ILLUSIONISTS

The great surprise of the current decorative painting revival has been the demand for large-scale murals and trompe l'œil effects. Suddenly the wall-as-picture has become an international status symbol, and painters specializing in this area of the decorative arts find themselves summoned, like djinns, to paint jungle scenery round swimming pools in Aldershot, classical ruins on palace walls in Dubai, garlanded goddesses on ceilings in Paris or romantic landscapes in living-rooms in Miami. What clients are re-discovering is that skilful painting can supply whatever element seems lacking in their surroundings. Most coveted, it seems, is a look of romantic, patrician decay; the newer the penthouse, the more gently crumbling the painted 'rustication', complete with moss, cracks, lizards and carved escutcheons, defaced by time.

The teasing inconsequence of trompe l'œil is brilliantly demonstrated in this kitchen, where almost nothing is what it seems and wisps of string on painted nails, objects dangling out of drawers, are a cleaning lady's despair. Amateurs could have fun with the idea of trompe l'œil objects on cupboard doors. Another fashionable use for trompe l'œil is the addition of architectural details to flat walls, like this arched niche.

Stepping through the front door can land you anywhere from the Temple of Diana to a geisha house or Tippoo Sahib's travelling war tent. If the trompe l'œil artist was in puckish mood, unsuspecting visitors may find their coats sliding off painted coat hooks, illusory ten pound notes might peep out from under the carpet or appear swept into a pile on the hearth, cigarette packets on the table may mislead you into reaching for one, while painted mice scuttle into painted mouseholes. Paul and Janet Czainskis spend a few weeks in Scotland each summer adding yet another hallucinatory detail, such as a field-mouse clinging to a wheat stalk, a dragon-fly or dandelion, to an astonishing bedroom where the forces of nature seem to be fighting to gain admission through every painted crack and crevice, a *tour de force* of what admirers of the Gothick called 'horrid imagination'. Whatever this painted phantasmagoria may indicate about its patrons, it is all in a day's work for the artists who create them: 'Turps smells the same whether you're in Bangkok or Tuscany', as one of them put it.

Trompe l'œil work at the level on which Ian Cairnie, the Czainskis, Lincoln Taber and their colleagues operate, is technically highly skilled, and probably beyond most amateurs. Unless the painted mouse really 'deceives the eye' the joke misfires. On the other hand, a slightly primitive version of trompe l'œil can be decorative and witty in the right place. Painting the contents of cupboards on their doors, as in the Czainskis' example shown here, is an attractive way of reminding people where to stow things after washing-up. 'You use just about every trick there is to speed things up, it's not like conventional easel painting in that sense. Stencils, graining, stippling, anything is used that will help the illusion along.' Or, like Victoria Sharples, you can have fun painting alarm clocks and chamber pots on bedside-cupboard doors, and sheafs of trompe

l'œil correspondence on the breakast tray. Small faked details like these are fun to paint, and add an amusing personal note. The only way to do them is to scale, with the objects in front of you so that you can reproduce them faithfully. Getting the shadows right is the secret of success, Paul Czainskis says, because it is shadow that gives the flat painted article a three-dimensional look. He will scrumple a ten pound note to create shadows before painting its portrait. Ian Cairnie lays stress on getting little details exactly right. 'If you are doing a trompe door, you need to take time over the knob, the keyhole and the hinges. If they look convincing you are halfway there.' When he painted a trompe window, framing a Claude Lorraine view, in a client's windowless hall, he took twice as long painting the glazing bars as the pastoral vista beyond.

One paint with which Owen Turville wants to experiment further, both for exterior and interior murals, is the German-made Keim paint, sold here to the trade by Mineral Protect Ltd. The principle behind the Keim paint was discovered over a century ago by Professor Keim who was looking for a paint with the lasting qualities of true fresco. The oldest Keim-painted surfaces are over a hundred years old and look pristine, so it looks as if he was successful. The Keim system uses natural earth oxide pigments which are painted onto a mineral substrate and fixed by a silicate binder; the chemical reaction forms a crystalline surface, which not only prevents colours fading but allows surfaces to breathe, ideal for damp walls or places with condensation problems. The only problem with Keim paint is that it cannot be applied over a previously painted surface, other than limewash. It can be used straight onto standard thistle plaster, however, or over concrete.

For mural painters Keim is made in a special formulation where the silicate binder is brushed on after the painting is complete. This allows changes to be made. The Keim system approaches the clear, luminous colour of true fresco. To achieve that colour quality over walls which are to be simply painted rather than 'muralised', the makers recommend using a combination method. Paint the walls first with white Granital, their exterior base, and then brush over a diluted colour mixed with half fixative, half water. It costs perhaps twice as much as a standard paint, but gives a freshness and subtlety of colour unattainable except by the laborious old fresco method, and will last virtually for ever.

At present Keim paints are largely used for restoration work, inside and out – the Queen Mother's house at Windsor has a Keim finish. Mineral Protect Ltd (see suppliers index) do not sell directly over the counter, but via architects and decorating firms, because they want to ensure that the paints are used over a properly prepared base of the right material.

Ashlar or painted stone work

It is something of a coup for us to be able to publish the first photographs of work by Paul and Janet Czainskis (see pp. 128–9), a highly talented young couple whose reputation has spread entirely by word of mouth. Paul painted the trompe stone-work in this tiny London hall using dry pigments – raw sienna, raw umber, white and vandyke brown – in stale beer, an old graining trick. To obviate brushmarks and achieve an air-brushed smoothness, he sponged the shading colours through a stencil, which allowed him to keep building up layers of watercolour until he got the effect he wanted. The highlights, or light edges of dressed stone, were done by wiping off the watercolour with a wet chamois to reveal the white base. Stencilling over in a paler colour obliterated the stencil ties, and the whole surface was finished in matt varnish.

Seeing is believing; there is something magical about transformations like these that appeals to the child in all of us. Paint can do so much for you if you just use a little 'paintability'. It can work miracles, and not only in this most spectacular form of decorative painting. Colour, texture and pattern can be yours – not only on the walls, but just about everywhere. All achieved with paint, and nothing but paint. I hope this book will stir your imaginations and provide the key to making your home a unique environment instead of just a 'painted box'.

RIGHT *This exercise in perspective, dated 1662 and painted by the Dutch painter Van Hoogstraeten, is a celebrated example of visual trickery, especially when seen through an enfilade of doorways as at Dyrham Park.*

FAR RIGHT *Graham Rust is one of the most full-blooded muralists around today, as evidenced in this rusticated hallway where the jungle seems to be taking over – notice the spectacular cracks.*

A trompe l'œil doorway uses a mixture of styles: grisaille for the architectural fantasy, and stunning realism for the odd painted details, like the monkey.

LEFT *More of the trompe l'œil painter's favourite witticisms for you to try – pillars and draperies.*

RIGHT *Caught in a beam of light, a flutter of brilliantly coloured trompe l'œil butterflies.*

DESIGNER IDEAS

66 Owen Turville worked for many years with John Fowler, and has absorbed much of the Fowler wisdom about colour, together with a painterly handling of decorative techniques. What he would really like to do is paint landscapes; in the meantime large-scale murals provide an outlet, though like most Fowler-trained decorative artists he can turn his hand to anything from restoring antique furniture to painting flowers on cushions.

'I find Liquitex [acrylic] gesso makes a marvellous primer for murals. I paint straight onto it, using acrylics as a rule for the drying speed, though I sometimes finish a mural in oils. I usually prepare a fairly finished coloured sketch of the scheme for the client, so I work from that. I might transpose it onto the wall surface very accurately to scale, making a grid – black cotton fixed in place with Blu-Tack is a good way of marking out a grid and it can be removed as soon as you have blocked in the design. Sometimes, though, I might start by drawing a large rough sketch using chalks or charcoal – pencil has a way of coming through paint. But my

favourite means of drawing a preparatory sketch is with a brush. A brush makes thin and thick lines, almost carving out the design, and I have another brush dipped in white spirit as an eraser. I suppose if you were a beginner you could project a picture onto the wall and draw round it. If I'm drawing with the brush I

might use a few colours, sienna for warm tones, umber and ultramarine for cool ones. But they would be very thin, almost monochrome, with just enough colour to give a suggestion of texture and tone. It's amazing how little you need to create an illusion – most people rush into mural painting and do too much too soon.'

'You need to keep the concept very broad. Go for the main areas of light and the main areas of dark – the middle tones come easily after that. When you've got the basic shapes right, you can superimpose your colours. Perspective is always a bother; one way round the problem is to go for a flat cartoon effect, a bit like a stencil. Keep the whole scheme simple and find variety in the textures. I usually paint on a white background but I think an amateur might get better results working on a coloured ground, a stony, raw sienna colour for instance, so that you are drawing in lighter or darker tones. Having a base colour unifies everything and makes it all look as if it was flooded with a certain light. Most murals are probably better varnished, but it depends on the context. Liquitex also make a good acrylic varnish, which comes in a matt and gloss finish, but you can usually get the degree of shine you want by intermixing.' **"**

SUPPLIERS INDEX

Most paint stores carry a basic range of latex paints, enamels, and tinting colors; below are listed suppliers of more specialized items, which might be harder to find.

S. Wolf's Sons, 771 9th Avenue, New York, New York 10019, stock a complete range of specialist painting supplies, including artists' colors, specialist brushes, bulletin colors, rabbit skin glue, whiting, glazing liquids, wood stains and bleaches, gold leaf and Keim paints. They have a catalogue available, and will ship anywhere in the USA or Canada.

Artists' supplies such as oil colors, dry artists' colors and metallic powders can be obtained from:

Arthur Brown & Bro., 2 West 46th Street, New York, New York 10036.

Sam Flax, Corporate Offices at 111 8th Avenue, New York, New York 10011; branches throughout the States.

H. Behlen & Bro., Route 30 North, Amsterdam, New York 12020 specialize in wood finish supplies, and stock a range of spirit- and water-based stains, and wood bleaches.

Adele Bishop, PO Box 3349, Kinston, North Carolina 28501 can supply everything needed for stencilling.

The Chromatic Paint Corporation, PO Box 105, Garnerville, New York, New York 10923 manufacture a range of Japan colors and bulletin colors.

Hammill & Gillespie, 154 South Livingstone Avenue, Livingstone, New Jersey 07039, are importers of whiting.

Hamilton Brush (USA), PO Box 5176, Westport, Connecticut 06881, have an extensive range of specialist brushes.

McCloskey Varnish Company, 7600 State Road, Philadelphia, Pennsylvania 19136, are manufacturers of glazing liquids.

Mineros Industries, 505 West 211th Street, New York, New York 10034, are importers of Keim paints.

M. Swift & Son, PO Box 150, Hartford, Connecticut 06101 manufacture gold leaf.

SELECT BIBLIOGRAPHY

J. Itten, **The Elements of Colour**, New York, Van Nostrad Reinhold, 1971

Lorraine Johnson, **The New Decorators' Directory**, London, Michael Joseph, 1985

Ralph Mayer, **The Artists' Handbook of Materials and Techniques**, London, Faber & Faber, 1982

Isabel O'Neil, **The Art of the Painted Finish,** New York, William Morrow & Company, Inc., 1971

Mario Praz, **An Illustrated History of Interior Decoration**, London, Thames & Hudson, 1982

Janet Waring, **Early American Stencils on Walls and Furniture**, New York, Dover, 1968

GLOSSARY

stainers tinting colors or colorizers
emulsion latex paint
glaze glazing liquid
filler spackle
palette knife spackling knife
white spirit mineral spirit
Clingfilm Saran wrap
wood filler wood putty
knotting knot sealer
primer then undercoat use an enamel
undercoater only
gloss enamel paint

methylated spirits denatured alcohol
cornflour cornstarch
cotton wool absorbent cotton
chemist druggist
signwriters' paint bulletin color
drawing pins thumb tacks
atomizer diffuser
Plasticine modelling clay
flat paint alkyd flat paint
flat emulsion and matt vinyl paint latex flap
paint and latex flat enamel
vinyl enamel latex enamel

PICTURE ACKNOWLEDGEMENTS

Illustrations have been reproduced by kind permission of the following:

The American Museum in Britain, Bath: 148 top & bottom, 149 left & right
Barbara Broun (artist): 72 top, 73 (photos: Miriam Reik)
Bridgeman Art Library: 9 top

Cosmopolitan: 21 (photo: Tony Chau)
Davies, Keeling & Trowbridge: 176 top, back cover bottom right
Dragons: 133
Elizabeth Whiting & Associates: 24 bottom
Christine Hanscombe: 80 top

Homes & Gardens: 60/61 (artist: Alison Munro)
Jocasta Innes: 116, 124 top, 125, 176 (artist: Paul Czainskis; photos: Sarah Ryder-Richardson)
Ken Kirkwood: 182/183, 183
Leonard Lassalle (artist): 96, 97 top & bottom, 112/113 top & bottom (photos: J. Fieldwick)
Karen Mander: 6 (photo: Tim Beddows)
Meridien: 156 top right
Derry Moore: 80 bottom (artist: Owen Turville), 88 top & bottom, 137
James Mortimer: 81
The National Trust Photographic Library: 8 bottom (photo: John Bethell), 180
Ronald Sheridan's Photo-Library: 6 top
Stewart Walton: 108 bottom left (photo: Glynn Bristow)

Carolyn Warrender: 108 centre (artist: Jim Smart)
Jeremy Whitaker: 181, 182 (artist: Graham Rust)
William Morris Gallery, Walthamstow, London: 12
The World of Interiors: 13 (Cecil Higgins Museum, Bedford; photo: Lucinda Lambton), 84 top & bottom, 85 (photos: Bill Batten), 104, 105 (photos: James Wedge), 136 (photo: Clive Frost), 172 top left (photo: Peter Wolessynski), 173 (photo: James Mortimer)

Weidenfeld & Nicolson Archives:
photo: Wendy Bird [Goodsports]/John Aparicio: 161 bottom right (artist: Naomi Colvin)

photo: Rick Kemp: 113, 144 top, 152 top & bottom, 153, 156 top left, bottom left & bottom right, 160 top left & right, 161 top right, 168, 169, 172 bottom left, 185 right, 192

photo: Chris Ridley: 132, 144 bottom, 161 left

photo: Fritz von der Schulenberg: frontispiece, 1, 16, 17, 20, 24 top (artist: Nemone Burgess), 45, 48 top (artist Nemone Burgess), 48 bottom, 57, 64, 65 top & bottom (artist: Jim Smart), 92, 93 top & bottom, 100, 101, 108 top right & bottom right, 109, 120, 120/121, 121, 124 bottom, 128, 129, 132, 140, 141, 157, 160 bottom left, 172 top right & bottom right, 187

photo: Jeremy Whitaker: 72 bottom, 184, 184/185

Artwork was produced by Stewart Walton

INDEX

Page numbers in *italic* refer to illustrations. Where illustration and caption appear on different pages, the reference is to the page bearing the caption.

ACKNOWLEDGEMENTS

People helped in so many ways during the preparation of this book: with ideas, information, encouragement. Shane Watson was my lifeline, researching, classifying; Emma Hardy and Thomas Lane brought both painting skills and unquenchable good humour; Sally Kenny not only invented new and distinctive finishes but also explained them lucidly. I am endlessly indebted to the many decorative painters who shared their time, enthusiasm and insights, and shined up their subjects all over again. They speak for themselves in the book, but I would like to give them a big extra thank you here: to Peter Miall for an inspiring day driving round Kent; to Stewart Walton for allowing himself to be enthused about stencils, rubber stamps and 'panels'; to Jeffrey Ratcliffe for many a telephone briefing session, and particularly to the patient and talented team at Weidenfelds – to Denny for coping with copy, the design team for an inspired layout, and Lucy for making so many phone calls, my warmest thanks.

Published in the United States by
Harmony Books, a division of Crown Publishers, Inc.,
225 Park Avenue South, New York, New York 10003

Originally published in Great Britain in 1986 by George Weidenfeld & Nicolson Limited,
91 Clapham High Street, London SW4 7TA

HARMONY and colophon are trademarks of Crown Publishers Inc.

Manufactured in Italy

Library of Congress Cataloging in Publication Data
Innes, Jocasta
Decorating with Paint
Includes index
1. House painting—amateurs' manuals. 2. Interior decoration—amateurs' manuals.
3. Decoration and ornament. I. Title.
TT323.I55 1986   698'.14   86-4793
ISBN 0-517-57229-X

10 9 8 7 6 5 4 3 2 1

First American Paperback edition

OVERLEAF *Back view of my silent portrait,*
showing John Fisher's ingenious dog support.